NEW LONGMAN LITERATURE

Educating Rita

Willy Russell

Notes: John Shuttleworth

Edinburgh Gate
Harlow, Essex

Pearson Education Limited
Edinburgh Gate
Harlow
Essex
CM20 2JE
England

This educational edition first published 2000
Editorial notes © Pearson Education Limited 2000

ISBN 0 582 43445 9
Second impression 2001

Printed in Singapore (KHL)

The Publisher's policy is to use paper manufactured from sustainable
forests.

Designed and packaged by McLean Press Ltd
Cover illustration by Matthew Williams

Contents

Introduction

Educating the author by Willy Russell   1
Setting the scene   7
Main characters   7
Themes and ideas   8
Language and style   9

Educating Rita

Act 1 Scene 1 and notes   12
Scene 2 and notes   28
Scenes 3, 4 and notes   40
Scene 5 and notes   50
Scenes 6 and notes   58
Scenes 7, 8 and notes   64
Act 2 Scene 1 and notes   72
Scenes 2, 3 and notes   82
Scenes 4, 5 and notes   92
Scenes 6, 7 and notes   100

Further reading   106

Programme of study   109

Glossary   111

Introduction

Educating the author by Willy Russell

I was born in Whiston, which is just outside Liverpool. They talk funny in Whiston. To a Liverpudlian everyone else talks funny. Fortunately, when I was five my mum and dad moved to Knowsley, on to an estate full of Liverpudlians who taught me how to talk correctly.

My dad worked in a factory (later, having come to hate factory life, he got out and bought a chip shop) and my mother worked in a warehouse; in those days there was a common ritual called employment. I went to school just down the road from my grandma's mobile grocer's (it was in an old charabanc which had long since lost any chance of going anywhere but everyone called it the mobile).

In school I learned how to read very early. Apart from reading books I played football and kick-the-can and quite enjoyed the twice-weekly gardening lessons. We each had a plot and at the end of the summer term we could take home our turnips and lettuces and radish and stuff. We used to eat it on the way. Our headmaster (Pop Chandler) had a war wound in his leg and everyone said it was 'cause of the shrapnel. When we went to the baths (if he was in a good mood) he'd show us this hole in his leg. It was horrible. It was blue. We loved looking at it.

Other than reading books, gardening, playing football and looking at shrapnel wounds I didn't care much for school. I watched the telly a lot. Never went to any theatres or anything like that. Saw a show at the village hall once but it was all false. They talked funny and got married at the end. I only remember it 'cause I won the raffle, a box of fruit, with a coconut right in the middle. When we opened it the coconut stunk. It was bad.

When I was eleven they sent me to a secondary school in Huyton. Like all the other Knowsley kids I was frightened of Huyton. There were millions of new houses there and flats, and everyone said there were gangs with bike chains and broken bottles and truck spanners. What everyone said was right; playtime was nothing to do with play, it was about survival. Thugs roamed the concrete and casually destroyed anything that couldn't move fast enough. Dinner time was the same only four times as long.

If you were lucky enough to survive the food itself you then had to get out into the playground world of protection rackets, tobacco hustlers, trainee contract killers and plain no-nonsense sadists. And that's without the teachers!

Anders his name was, the metalwork teacher. All the other kids loved metalwork. First thing we had to do was file a small rectangle of metal so that all the sides were straight; this would then be name-stamped and used as a nameplate to identify each kid's work. I never completed mine. After a matter of weeks other kids had moved from making nameplates to producing anything from guns and daggers to boiler-room engines while it was obvious that I was never going to be able to get the sides of my piece of metal straight. Eventually it was just a sliver, a near perfect needle, though not straight. I showed it to him, Anders; I couldn't hide it from him any longer. He chucked it in the bin and wordlessly handed me another chunk of metal and indicated that I had to do it again and again and again until I did it *right!* And I did, for a whole school year, every metalwork lesson, I tried and failed and with every failure there came a chunk of metal and the instruction to do it again. I started to have terrible nightmares about Anders. It's the only time I can remember feeling real hatred for another human being.

After another year I moved school, to Rainford where it used to be countryside, where they all talked funny, where the thugs were rather old-fashioned, charming even. Whereas in Huyton you could be bike-chained to bits without warning, in Rainford the thugs observed some sort of manners: *Ey you, does t' want t' fight wi me?* You could still get hurt, of course, and some of the teachers were headcases; but there were no sadists, metalwork was not on the curriculum, there were fields and lawns in place of concrete playgrounds and compared to Huyton it was paradise. We even had a long lesson every week called 'silent reading'; just enter the classroom and pick up a book, start reading and as long as you made no noise you were left completely alone with the book. I remember clearly, during one of these lessons, locked into a novel, the sun streaming through the windows, experiencing the feeling of total peace and security and thinking what a great thing it must be to write books and create in people the sort of feeling the author had created in me. I wanted to be a writer!

It was a wonderful and terrible thought – wonderful because I sensed, I knew, it was the only thing for me. Terrible because how could I, a kid from the 'D' stream, a piece of factory fodder, ever change the course that my life was already set upon? How the hell could I ever be the sort of person who could become a writer? It was a shocking and ludicrous thought, one that I hid deep in myself for years, but one that would not go away.

During my last year at school they took us to a bottle-making factory in St Helens, me and all the other kids who were obviously factory types. I could feel the brutality of the place even before I entered its windowless walls. Inside, the din and the smell were overpowering. Human beings worked in there but the figures I saw, feeding huge and relentlessly hungry machines, seemed not to be a part of humanity but a part of the machinery itself. Those men who were fortunate enough not to have to work directly with the machinery, the supervisors, foremen I suppose, glared, prodded, occasionally shouted. Each one of them looked like Anders from the metalwork class.

Most of the kids with whom I visited that place accepted that it was their lot to end up in that place. Some even talked of the money they would earn and made out that they couldn't wait to get inside those walls.

But, in truth, I think they all dreaded it as much as I. Back in school I stared at the geography books I hadn't read, the history pages and science I hadn't studied, the maths books (which would still be a mystery today, even if I'd studied them from birth), and I realised that with only six months' schooling to go, I'd left it all hopelessly too late. Like it or not I'd end up in a factory. There was no point in trying to catch up with years of schoolwork in a mere six months. And so I didn't. The months I had left were spent sagging school and going to a dark underground club every lunchtime. It was called the Cavern and the smell of sweat in there was as pungent as any in a factory, the din was louder than any made by machines. But the sweat was mingled with cheap perfume and was produced by dancing and the noise was music, made by a group called the Beatles.

One afternoon in summer I left the Cavern after the lunchtime session and had to go to the Bluecoat Chambers to sit an examination, the result of which would determine how suited I was to become an apprentice printer. I didn't want to be an apprentice printer; I wanted to be back in the Cavern. I did the exam because my dad thought it would be a good thing. I answered the questions on how many men it would take to lift three tons of coal in seven hours if it took one man two minutes to lift a sack of coal on a rainy day etc. And I wrote the essay of my choice (titled *A Group Called the Beatles).* And I failed.

At home there were conferences, discussions, rows and slanging matches all on the same subject – me and the job I'd get. Eventually my mother resolved it all. She suggested I become a ladies' hairdresser! I can only think that a desire to have her hair done free must have clouded her normally reasonable mind. It was such a bizarre suggestion that I went along with it. I went to a college for a year or so and pretended to learn all about hairdressing. In reality most of my time was spent at parties or arranging parties.

It was a good year but when it ended I had to go to work. Someone was actually prepared to hire me as a hairdresser, to let me loose on the heads of innocent and unsuspecting customers. There were heads scalded during shampooing, heads which should have become blonde but turned out green, heads of Afro frizz (before Afro frizz had been invented) and heads rendered temporarily bald. Somehow, probably from moving from one shop to another before my legendary abilities were known, I survived. For six years I did a job I didn't understand and didn't like. Eventually I even had my own small salon and it was there that on slack days I would retire to the back room and try to do the one and only thing I felt I understood, felt that I could do: write.

I wrote songs mostly but tried, as well, to write sketches and poetry, even a book. But I kept getting interrupted by women who, reasonably enough on their part, wanted their hair done. It dawned upon me that if ever I was to become a writer I had first to get myself into the sort of world which allowed for, possibly even encouraged such aspiration. But that would mean a drastic change of course. Could I do it? Could I do something which those around me didn't understand? I would have to break away. People would be puzzled and hurt.

I compromised. I sensed that the world in which I would be able to write would be the academic world. Students have long holidays. I'd be able to spend a good part of the year writing and the other part learning to do a job, teaching perhaps, which would pay the rent. I wasn't qualified to train as a teacher but I decided to dip my toe in the water and test the temperature. I enrolled in a night class for O level English Literature and passed it.

To go to a college though, I'd need at least five O levels. Taking them at night school would take too long. I had to find a college which would let me take a full-time course, pack everything into one year. I found a college but no authority was prepared to give me a maintenance grant or even pay my fees. I knew I couldn't let the course go, knew I could survive from day to day – but how was I going to find the money to pay the fees? The hairdressing paid nothing worth talking of.

I heard of a job, a contract job in Fords, cleaning oil from the girders high above the machinery. With no safety equipment whatsoever and with oil on every girder the danger was obvious. But the money was big.

I packed up the hairdresser's and joined the night-shift girder cleaners. Some of them fell and were injured, some of them took one look at the job and walked away. Eventually there were just a few of us desperate or daft enough to take a chance.

I stayed in that factory just long enough to earn the fees I needed; no extras, nothing. Once I'd earned enough for the fees, I came down from the girders, collected my money and walked away. I enrolled at the college and one day in September made my way along the stone-walled drive.

The obvious difference in age between me and the sixteen-year-olds pouring down the drive made me feel exposed and nervous but as I entered the glass doors of Childwall College I felt as if I'd made it back to the beginning. I could start again. I felt at home.

Setting the scene

The main, indeed the only, setting for *Educating Rita* is in Frank's book-lined study in a university in northern England. All the action between Frank and Rita takes place in this study, although important events do occur offstage. Rita's visit to the university Summer School is one of these, as is her embarrassed attempt to attend a dinner party at Frank's house.

The play is set in the time that it was written, in 1985, and although this is in the fairly recent past, you will still need to be alert to some of the popular cultural references that Rita, in particular, uses. For example, at one point in Act 1 Scene 2, she compares Jane Austen, the nineteenth-century novelist, and Tracy Austin, a 1980s' tennis player. A modern audience, whilst they will have little difficulty in recognising Jane Austen, may well have forgotten just who Tracy Austin was.

Rita is a literature student at the Open University. This is a university that was founded in the 1960s as a way of enabling adult students, like Rita, who had never had the chance to go to university at the age of eighteen, to study for a degree without having to leave home. It has proved a very popular way of studying and has helped many people. Students learn via a combination of television and radio programmes, booklets, and by having regular meetings with a tutor. Frank, Rita's tutor, has a job at his own university, but does some part-time work teaching Open University students.

Main characters

Rita and Frank are the only two characters whom we see on stage, though other people are referred to by both of them. We hear about Denny, Rita's husband, about Julia, Frank's partner, and about Trish, Rita's flatmate, who attempts to kill herself. But it is Rita and Frank whom the audience gets to know best.

Rita is a working-class, twenty-six-year-old hairdresser who has taken the decisive step of enrolling on a literature course at the Open University. It has been a difficult decision as it means that she has to break away from the restrictions imposed on her by her husband and by the community in which she lives and works. Indeed, Rita's choice is a stark one: it is between starting a family, which Denny wants, or studying. In deciding to study and become more educated and culturally aware, Rita changes her life completely. She gradually becomes absorbed by culture and literature. It is only after her flatmate attempts suicide that she begins to realise that art and literature cannot provide all the answers. However, she decides to continue as a student and finally passes her examination.

Frank is a university lecturer in English Literature with a drink problem. He has had one failed marriage and his present relationship with Julia is not an easy one. However, he does appear to have a comfortable middle-class lifestyle and has achieved some minor success as a poet. His job, nevertheless, bores him and, in fact, by the end of the play, he has been sent away to Australia by the university authorities because of his drunken behaviour. Rita breezes into his life like a breath of fresh air; the story of the play is the story of their developing and changing relationships both as teacher and student and on a more personal level.

Themes and ideas

One of the main themes in the play has already been mentioned: personal relationships. The play focuses on the way that Rita and Frank influence each other. We see Rita developing during the course of the play. At the start, she is a nervous and cocky young woman who knows nothing about literature. We then see her become someone who acquires a superficial knowledge of the subject, but, by the end of the play, she has become a woman who is able to make wise and informed choices about the direction her life will take. Frank, on the other hand, does not really develop as much. Disillusioned and cynical at the start, the only progress he makes is downhill and, by the end of the play, he has effectively been dismissed from his post. At this point, Rita is about to embark on her new life, having passed her exams, whereas Frank is about to try to resurrect his career in Australia. Even his contact with the bright and chirpy Rita has failed to halt his decline. In their conversations with each other, they also reveal much about their unsatisfactory relationships with their partners, Denny and Julia.

The second major theme that Willy Russell deals with is the clash of cultures. Rita comes from a working-class society which she has grown to despise as she feels it is stifling her, although the play does show us that it can be quite a warm and close-knit community. It is a culture that knows and cares little about literature, though Frank tries to show Rita that it does have its own culture and values. Frank, on the other hand, inhabits a middle-class academic world in which literature is seen to be important, even though he himself seems to have grown tired of it. We learn about these two cultures from their conversations, though you may need to consult the notes to understand fully Frank's literary references and Rita's to 1980s' popular culture. Of course, you would not be alone, as neither Rita nor Frank always understands the other's remarks, particularly in the early scenes of the play. Rita is, however, determined to acquire middle-class culture and she sees education as the means to achieve this aim.

Language and style
One of the most appealing features of *Educating Rita* for theatre audiences and readers alike is that it is a very amusing and entertaining play. Much of this stems from the way the two characters talk. Not only do they not always pick up each other's cultural references, but also sometimes it is as if they are speaking

different languages. Rita speaks colloquially (in everyday, local language) and has a working-class accent, though for a short while in Act 2 Scene 2 she attempts to change it and to 'talk properly'. She soon, however, reverts to her normal voice. Frank, in contrast, speaks in standard English and, as far as we can tell from the printed page, without any noticeable accent. Rita's lively and irreverent speech is a source of humour, as is the interplay and repartee between her and Frank. Willy Russell makes their discussions, even of the most serious issues, engaging and entertaining.

Educating Rita

Notes for Act 1 Scene 1

A playwright has a lot to do in the first scene of a play. He has got to introduce us to some of, if not all, the characters; he has to let us know something of their background and relationship with each other; he may introduce some of the main themes of his play. He has also to show when and where the play is set and, of course, most important of all, he has to interest and entertain his audience.

What do you think?

As you read or act this first scene, think about your impressions of the two characters: do you think you are going to enjoy meeting them in the rest of the play? Think about:

- the possible ways the relationship between Frank and Rita might develop
- how Willy Russell gives us information about each of them.

Questions

See if you can find evidence in this scene to answer the following questions:

1. Why does Rita want to study?
2. What suggests to you that she is not a stupid woman?
3. What do we learn about Frank's relationship with Julia?
4. What does Frank think of his job?
5. What shows that Frank and Rita do not always understand each other?

Further activity

Write Rita's letter of application to become a student at the Open University. Make sure that you include not only the reasons she gives for wanting to study and why she thinks she might be suitable, but also something about her background and educational qualifications. You'll have to look at other parts of the play for some of these details. You may want to set part of the letter like a curriculum vitae (CV), a formal list of her qualifications and experience so far. Sometimes, letters of application are supported by the comments of one or two referees who have known the person for some time. Write the references that Rita's headteacher and her boss at the hairdresser's might give her. Remember that Rita won't see these references, as they are confidential.

12

Act 1 Scene 1

A room on the first floor of a Victorian-built university in the north of England

There is a large bay window LEFT *with a desk placed in front of it and another desk* CENTRE *covered with various papers and books. The walls are lined with books and on one wall hangs a good print of a nude religious scene*

When the curtain rises FRANK, *who is in his early fifties, is standing* DOWN RIGHT CENTRE *holding an empty mug. He goes to the bookcases* DOWN RIGHT *and starts taking books from the shelves, hurriedly replacing them before moving on to another section*

FRANK *(looking along the shelves)* Where the hell …? Eliot? *(He pulls out some books and looks into the bookshelf)* No. *(He replaces the books)* 'E' *(He thinks for a moment)* 'E', 'e' 'e' … *Suddenly he remembers)* Dickens. *(Jubilantly he moves to the Dickens section and pulls out a pile of books to reveal a bottle of whisky. He takes the bottle from the shelf and goes to the small table by the door and pours himself a large slug into the mug in his hand)*

The telephone rings and startles him slightly. He manages a gulp at the whisky before he picks up the receiver and although his speech is not slurred, we should recognize the voice of a man who shifts a lot of booze

Yes? … Of course I'm still here. … Because I've got this Open University woman coming, haven't I? … Tch … Of course I told you. … But darling, you shouldn't have prepared dinner should you? Because I said, I distinctly remember saying that I would be late … Yes. Yes, I probably shall go to the pub afterwards. I shall need to go to the pub afterwards. I shall need to wash

13

away the memory of some silly woman's attempts to get into the mind of Henry James or whoever it is we're supposed to study on this course. ... Oh God, why did I take this on? ... Yes. ... Yes I suppose I did take it on to pay for the drink. ... Oh, for God's sake, what is it? ... Yes, well – erm – leave it in the oven. ... Look if you're trying to induce some feeling of guilt in me over the prospect of a burnt dinner you should have prepared something other than lamb and ratatouille. ... Because, darling, I like my lamb done to the point of abuse and even I know that ratatouille cannot be burned. ... Darling, you could incinerate ratatouille and still it wouldn't burn. ... What do you mean am I determined to go to the pub? I don't need determination to get me into a pub ...

There is a knock at the door

Look, I'll have to go. ... There's someone at the door. ... Yes, yes I promise. ... Just a couple of pints. ... Four. ...

There is another knock at the door

(Calling in the direction of the door) Come in! *(He continues on the telephone)* Yes. ... All right ... yes. ... Bye, bye. ... *(He replaces the receiver)* Yes, that's it, you just pop off and put your head in the oven. *(Shouting)* Come in! Come in!

The door swings open revealing RITA

RITA *(from the doorway)* I'm comin' in, aren't I? It's that stupid bleedin' handle on the door. You wanna get it fixed! *(She comes into the room)*

FRANK *(staring, slightly confused)* Erm – yes, I suppose I always mean to ...

RITA *(going to the chair by the desk and dumping her bag)* Well that's no good always meanin' to, is it? Y' should get on with it; one of these days you'll be shoutin' 'Come in' an' it'll go on forever because the poor sod on the other side won't be able to get in. An' you won't be able to get out.

FRANK *stares at* RITA *who stands by the desk*

FRANK You are?

14

RITA What am I?

FRANK Pardon?

RITA What?

FRANK *(looking for the admission papers)* Now you are?

RITA I'm a what?

FRANK *looks up and then returns to the papers as* RITA *goes to hang her coat on the door hooks*

RITA *(noticing the picture)* That's a nice picture, isn't it? *(She goes up to it)*

FRANK Erm – yes, I suppose it is – nice …

RITA *(studying the picture)* It's very erotic.

FRANK *(looking up)* Actually I don't think I've looked at it for about ten years, but yes, I suppose it is.

RITA There's no suppose about it. Look at those tits.

He coughs and goes back to looking for the admission paper

Is it supposed to be erotic? I mean when he painted it do y' think he wanted to turn people on?

FRANK Erm – probably.

RITA I'll bet he did y' know. Y' don't paint pictures like that just so that people can admire the brush strokes, do y'?

FRANK *(giving a short laugh)* No – no – you're probably right.

RITA This was the pornography of its day, wasn't it? It's sort of like *Men Only*, isn't it? But in those days they had to pretend it wasn't erotic so they made it religious, didn't they? Do *you* think it's erotic?

FRANK *(taking a look)* I think it's very beautiful.

RITA I didn't ask y' if it was beautiful.

FRANK But the term 'beautiful' covers the many feelings I have about that picture, including the feeling that, yes, it is erotic.

RITA *(coming back to the desk)* D' y' get a lot like me?

FRANK Pardon?

RITA Do you get a lot of students like me?

FRANK Not exactly, no …

RITA I was dead surprised when they took me. I don't suppose they would have done if it'd been a proper university. The Open University's different though, isn't it?

FRANK I've erm – not had much more experience of it than you. This is the first O. U. work I've done.

RITA D' y' need the money?

FRANK I do as a matter of fact.

RITA It's terrible these days, the money, isn't it? With the inflation an' that. You work for the ordinary university, don't y'? With the real students. The Open University's different, isn't it?

FRANK It's supposed to embrace a more comprehensive studentship, yes.

RITA *(inspecting a bookcase)* Degrees for dishwashers.

FRANK Would you – erm – would you like to sit down?

RITA No! Can I smoke? *(She goes to her bag and rummages in it)*

FRANK Tobacco?

RITA Yeh. *(She half-laughs)* Was that a joke? *(She takes out a packet of cigarettes and a lighter)* Here – d' y' want one? *(She takes out two cigarettes and dumps the packet on the desk)*

FRANK *(after a pause)* Ah – I'd love one.

RITA Well, have one.

FRANK *(after a pause)* I – don't smoke – I made a promise not to smoke.

RITA Well, I won't tell anyone.

FRANK Promise?

As FRANK *goes to take the cigarette* RITA *whips it from his reach*

RITA *(doing a Brownie salute)* On my oath as an ex Brownie. *(She gives him the cigarette)* I hate smokin' on me own. An' everyone seems to have packed up these days. *(She lights the cigarettes)* They're all afraid of gettin' cancer.

FRANK *looks dubiously at his cigarette*

RITA But they're all cowards.

FRANK Are they?

RITA You've got to challenge death an' disease. I read this poem about fightin' death …

FRANK Ah – Dylan Thomas …

RITA No. Roger McGough. It was about this old man who runs away from hospital an' goes out on the ale. He gets pissed an' stands in the street shoutin' an' challengin' death to come out an' fight. It's dead good.

FRANK Yes. I don't think I know the actual piece you mean …

RITA I'll bring y' the book – it's great.

FRANK Thank you.

RITA You probably won't think it's any good.

FRANK Why?

RITA It's the sort of poetry you can understand.

FRANK Ah. I see.

RITA *begins looking idly round the room*

FRANK Can I offer you a drink?

RITA What of?

FRANK Scotch?

RITA *(going to the bookcase* UP RIGHT*)* Y' wanna be careful with that stuff it kills y' brain cells.

FRANK But you'll have one? *(He gets up and goes to the small table)*

RITA All right. It'll probably have a job findin' my brain.

FRANK *(pouring the drinks)* Water?

RITA *(looking at the bookcase)* Yeh, all right. *(She takes a copy of 'Howards End' from the shelf)* What's this like?

FRANK *goes over to* RITA*, looks at the title of the book and then goes back to the drinks*

FRANK *Howards End*?

RITA Yeh. It sounds filthy, doesn't it? E. M. Foster.

FRANK Forster.

RITA Oh yeh. What's it like?

FRANK Borrow it. Read it.

RITA Ta. I'll look after it. (*She moves back towards the desk*) If I pack the course in I'll post it to y'.

FRANK *comes to the desk with drinks*

FRANK (*handing her the mug*) Pack it in? Why should you do that?

RITA *puts her drink down on the desk and puts the copy of 'Howards End' in her bag*

RITA I just might. I might decide it was a soft idea.

FRANK (*looking at her*) Mm. Cheers. If – erm – if you're already contemplating 'packing it in', why did you enrol in the first place?

RITA Because I wanna know.

FRANK What do you want to know?

RITA Everything.

FRANK Everything? That's rather a lot, isn't it? Where would you like to start?

RITA Well, I'm a student now, aren't I? I'll have to do exams, won' I?

FRANK Yes. Eventually.

RITA I'll have to learn about it all, won' I? Yeh. It's like y' sit there, don't y', watchin' the ballet or the opera on the telly an' – an' y' call it rubbish cos that's what it looks like? Cos y' don't understand. So y' switch it off an' say, that's fuckin' rubbish.

FRANK Do you?

RITA I do. But I don't want to. I wanna see. Y' don't mind me swearin', do y'?

FRANK Not at all.

RITA Do you swear?

FRANK Never stop.

RITA See, the educated classes know it's only words, don't they? It's only the masses who don't understand. I do it to shock them sometimes. Y' know when I'm in the hairdresser's – that's where I work – I'll say somethin' like, 'Oh, I'm really fucked', y' know, dead loud. It doesn't half cause a fuss.

18

FRANK Yes – I'm sure …

RITA But it doesn't cause any sort of fuss with educated people, does it? Cos they know it's only words and they don't worry. But these stuck-up idiots I meet, they think they're royalty just cos they don't swear; an' I wouldn't mind but it's the aristocracy that swears more than anyone, isn't it? They're effin' an' blindin' all day long. It's all 'Pass me the fackin' grouse' with them, isn't it? But y' can't tell them that round our way. It's not their fault; they can't help it. *(She goes to the window and looks out)* But sometimes I hate them. God, what's it like to be free?

FRANK Ah. Now there's a question. Will you have another drink? *(He goes to the small table)*

RITA *(shaking her head)* If I'd got some other tutor I wouldn't have stayed.

FRANK *(pouring himself a drink)* What sort of other tutor?

RITA Y' know, someone who objected to swearin'.

FRANK How did you know I wouldn't object?

RITA I didn't. I was just testin' y'.

FRANK *(coming back to the desk and looking at her)* Yes. You're doing rather a lot of that, aren't you?

RITA That's what I do. Y' know, when I'm nervous.

FRANK *(sitting in the swivel chair)* And how am I scoring so far?

RITA Very good, ten out of ten go to the top of the class an' collect a gold star. I love this room. I love that window. Do you like it?

FRANK What?

RITA The window.

FRANK I don't often consider it actually. I sometimes get an urge to throw something through it.

RITA What?

FRANK A student usually.

RITA *(smiling)* You're bleedin' mad you, aren't y'?

FRANK Probably.

Pause

RITA Aren't you supposed to be interviewin' me?

FRANK *(looking at the drink)* Do I need to?

RITA I talk too much, don't I? I know I talk a lot. I don't at home. I hardly ever talk when I'm there. But I don't often get the chance to talk to someone like you; to talk at you. D' y' mind?

FRANK Would you be at all bothered if I did?

She shakes her head and then turns it into a nod

I don't mind. *(He takes a sip of his drink)*

RITA What does assonance mean?

FRANK *(half spluttering)* What? *(He gives a short laugh)*

RITA Don't laugh at me.

FRANK No. Erm – assonance. Well, it's a form of rhyme. What's a – what's an example – erm – ? Do you know Yeats?

RITA The wine lodge?

FRANK Yeats the poet.

RITA No.

FRANK Oh. Well – there's a Yeats poem, called 'The Wild Swans at Coole'. In it he rhymes the word 'swan' with the word 'stone'. There, you see, an example of assonance.

RITA Oh. It means gettin' the rhyme wrong.

FRANK *(looking at her and laughing)* I've never really looked at it like that. But yes, yes you could say it means getting the rhyme wrong; but purposefully, in order to achieve a certain effect.

RITA Oh. *(There is a pause and she wanders round)* There's loads I don't know.

FRANK And you want to know everything?

RITA Yeh.

FRANK *nods and then takes her admission paper from his desk and looks at it*

FRANK What's your name?

RITA *(moving towards the bookcase)* Rita.

20

FRANK *(looking at the paper)* Rita. Mm. It says here Mrs S. White.

RITA *goes to the right of* FRANK, *takes a pencil, leans over and scratches out the initial 'S'*

RITA That's 'S' for Susan. It's just me real name. I've changed it to Rita, though. I'm not a Susan anymore. I've called meself Rita – y' know, after Rita Mae Brown.

FRANK Who?

RITA Y' know, Rita Mae Brown who wrote *Rubyfruit Jungle?* Haven't y' read it? It's a fantastic book. D' y' wanna lend it?

FRANK I'd – erm – I'd be very interested.

RITA All right.

RITA *gets a copy of 'Rubyfruit Jungle' from her bag and gives it to* FRANK. *He turns it over and reads the blurb on the back cover* What's your name?

FRANK Frank.

RITA Oh. Not after Frank Harris?

FRANK Not after Frank anyone.

RITA Maybe y' parents named y' after the quality. *(She sits in the chair by the desk)*

FRANK *puts down 'Rubyfruit Jungle'*

RITA Y' know Frank, Frank Ness, Elliot's brother.

FRANK What?

RITA I'm sorry – it was a joke. Y' know, Frank Ness, Elliot's brother.

FRANK *(bemused)* Ah.

RITA You've still not got it, have y'? Elliot Ness – y' know, the famous Chicago copper who caught Al Capone.

FRANK Ah. When you said Elliot I assumed you meant T. S. Eliot.

RITA Have you read his stuff?

FRANK Yes.

RITA All of it?

FRANK Every last syllable.

RITA *(impressed)* Honest? I couldn't even get through one poem. I tried to read this thing he wrote called 'J. Arthur Prufrock'; I couldn't finish it.

FRANK 'J. Alfred'.

RITA What?

FRANK I think you'll find it was 'J. Alfred Prufrock', Rita. J. Arthur is something else altogether.

RITA Oh yeh. I never thought of that. I've not half got a lot to learn, haven't I?

FRANK *(looking at her paper)* You're a ladies' hairdresser?

RITA Yeh.

FRANK Are you good at it?

RITA *(getting up and wandering around)* I am when I wanna be. Most of the time I don't want to though. They get on me nerves.

FRANK Who?

RITA The women. They never tell y' things that matter. Like, y' know, doin' a perm, well y' can't use a strong perm lotion on a head that's been bleached with certain sorts of cheap bleach. It makes all the hair break off. But at least once a month I'll get a customer in for a perm who'll swear to God that she's not had any bleach on; an' I can tell, I mean I can see it. So y' go ahead an' do the perm an' she comes out the drier with half an inch of stubble.

FRANK And what do you do about it?

RITA Try and sell them a wig.

FRANK My God.

RITA Women who want their hair doin', they won't stop at anythin', y' know. Even the pensioners are like that, y' know; a pensioner'll come in an' she won't tell y' that she's got a hearin' aid: so y' start cuttin' don't y'? Next thing – snip – another granny deaf for a fortnight. I'm always cuttin' hearin' aid cords. An' ear lobes.

FRANK You sound like something of a liability.

RITA I am. But they expect too much. They walk in the

22

hairdresser's an' an hour later they wanna walk out a different person. I tell them I'm a hairdresser, not a plastic surgeon. It's worse when there's a fad on, y' know like Farrah Fawcett Majors.

FRANK Who?

RITA Far-rah Fawcett Majors. Y' know, she used to be with *Charlie's Angels*.

FRANK *remains blank*

RITA It's a telly programme on ITV.

FRANK Ah.

RITA *(wandering towards the door)* You wouldn't watch ITV though, would y'? It's all BBC with you, isn't it?

FRANK Well, I must confess …

RITA It's all right, I know. Soon as I walked in here I said to meself, 'Y' can tell he's a Flora man'.

FRANK A what?

RITA A Flora man.

FRANK Flora? Flowers?

RITA *(coming back to the desk)* No, Flora, the bleedin' margarine, no cholesterol; it's for people like you who eat pebble-dashed bread, y' know the bread, with little hard hits in it, just like pebble-dashin'.

FRANK *(realizing and smiling)* Ah – pebble-dashed bread.

RITA Quick? He's like lightnin'. But these women, you see, they come to the hairdresser's cos they wanna be changed. But if you want to change y' have to do it from the inside, don't y'? Know like I'm doin'. Do y' think I'll be able to do it?

FRANK Well, it really depends on you, on how committed you are. Are you sure that you're absolutely serious about wanting to learn?

RITA I'm dead serious. Look, I know I take the piss an' that but I'm dead serious really. I take the piss because I'm not, y' know, confident like, but I wanna be, honest.

23

He nods and looks at her. She becomes uncomfortable and moves away a little

Tch. What y' lookin' at me for?

FRANK Because – I think you're marvellous. Do you know, I think you're the first breath of air that's been in this room for years.

RITA *(wandering around)* Tch. Now who's taking the piss?

FRANK Don't you recognize a compliment?

RITA Go way …

FRANK Where to?

RITA Don't be soft. Y' know what I mean.

FRANK What I want to know is what is it that's suddenly led you to this?

RITA What? Comin' here?

FRANK Yes.

RITA It's not sudden.

FRANK Ah.

RITA I've been realizin' for ages that I was, y' know, slightly out of step. I'm twenty-six. I should have had a baby by now; everyone expects it. I'm sure me husband thinks I'm sterile. He was moanin' all the time, y' know, 'Come off the pill, let's have a baby'. I told him I'd come off it, just to shut him up. But I'm still on it. *(She moves round to* FRANK*)* See, I don't wanna baby yet. See, I wanna discover meself first. Do you understand that?

FRANK Yes.

RITA *(moving to the chair* UP *of the desk and fiddling with it)* Yeh. They wouldn't round our way. They'd think I was mental. I've tried to explain it to me husband but between you an' me I think he's thick. No, he's not thick, he's blind, he doesn't want to see. You know if I'm readin', or watchin' somethin' different on the telly he gets dead narked. I used to just tell him to piss off but then I realized that it was no good doin' that, that I had to explain to him. I tried to explain that I wanted a better way of livin' me life. An' he listened to me. But he didn't understand because when I'd finished he said he agreed with me and that we should start savin' the money to move off our estate an' get a house out in Formby. Even if it was a new house I wanted I wouldn't go an' live in Formby. I hate that hole, don't you?

FRANK Yes.

RITA Where do you live?

FRANK Formby.

RITA *(sitting)* Oh.

FRANK *(getting up and going to the small table)* Another drink? *She shakes her head*

You don't mind if I do? *(He pours himself a drink)*

RITA No. It's your brain cells y' killin'.

FRANK *(smiling)* All dead long ago I'm afraid. *(He drinks)*

RITA *gets up and goes to Frank's chair. She plays with the swivel and then leans on it*

RITA When d' y' actually, y' know, start teaching me?

FRANK *(looking at her)* What can I teach you?

RITA Everything.

FRANK *leans on the filing cabinet, drinks, shakes his head and looks at her*

FRANK I'll make a bargain with you. Yes? I'll tell you everything I know – but if I do that you must promise never to come back here … You see I never – I didn't actually want to take this course in the first place. I allowed myself to be talked into it. I knew it was wrong. Seeing you only confirms my suspicion. My dear, it's not your fault, just the luck of the draw that you got me; but get me you did. And the thing is, between you, me and the walls, I'm actually an appalling teacher. *(After a pause)* Most of the time, you see, it doesn't actually matter – appalling teaching is quite in order for most of my appalling students. And the others manage to get by despite me. But you're different. You want a lot, and I can't give it. *(He moves towards her)* Everything I know – and you must listen to this – is that I know absolutely nothing. I don't like the hours, you know.

25

(He goes to the swivel chair and sits) Strange hours for this Open University thing. They expect us to teach when the pubs are open. I can be a good teacher when I'm in the pub, you know. Four pints of weak Guinness and I can be as witty as Wilde. I'm sorry – there are other tutors – I'll arrange it for you … post it on … *(He looks at her)*

RITA *slowly turns and goes towards the door. She goes out and quietly closes the door behind her. Suddenly the door bursts open and* RITA *flies in*

RITA *(going up to him)* Wait a minute, listen to me. Listen: I'm on this course, you are my teacher – an' you're gonna bleedin' well teach me.

FRANK There are other tutors – I've told you …

RITA You're my tutor. I don't want another tutor.

FRANK For God's sake, woman – I've told you …

RITA You're my tutor.

FRANK But I've told you – I don't want to do it. Why come to me?

RITA *(looking at him)* Because you're a crazy mad piss artist who wants to throw his students through the window, an' I like you. *(After a pause)* Don't you recognize a compliment?

FRANK Do you think I could have a cigarette?

RITA *(offering the packet of cigarettes)* I'll bring me scissors next week and give y' a haircut.

FRANK You're not coming here next week.

RITA *(lighting his cigarette)* I am. And you're gettin' y' hair cut.

FRANK I am not getting my hair cut.

RITA *(getting her bag)* I suppose y' wanna walk round like that, do y'? *(She goes towards the door)*

FRANK Like what?

RITA *(getting her coat)* Like a geriatric hippie.

Black out

RITA *exits*

Notes for Act 1 Scene 2

Rita returns for a tutorial with Frank the following week, having written her first piece of work on *Rubyfruit Jungle* for him. He finds it rather unsatisfactory. We learn more about their backgrounds and personal lives during the course of the tutorial and their relationship begins to develop, each warming towards the other.

What do you think?

Education is one of the central themes of the play, obviously, and the discussions in the scene frequently focus on the topic. Rita recounts some of her experiences at school and is determined to make Frank give her the education she feels she has missed. As you read the scene, try to identify:

- the lessons you think Rita really needs to learn
- whether Frank is a good teacher.

Questions

Think about the answers to these questions. Remember always to justify your views by referring to the text.

1. What is the significance of Rita oiling Frank's door?
2. What does she think about Frank's room and about the 'proper' students?
3. What more have you learned about Rita's background and education?
4. Why doesn't Frank like Rita's first essay?
5. Was Frank upset when his wife left him?

Further activity

You will have noticed that Willy Russell makes Rita and Frank speak differently from one another. In what way is it different? Basing your work on this scene and on the previous one, begin a chart called 'Rita's language'. Have two columns headed *Slang/Colloquial Words* and *Local Accent* and fill in the columns each time Rita uses an example of these in her speech. You could word-process this if you like. What does the chart tell you about her language? Is it different from standard English or is it casual standard English spoken with a local accent?

Scene 2

The lights come up on FRANK *who is standing in the centre of the room. He glances at his watch, moves to the window, looks out, glances at his watch again and then moves across to the books. He glances at his watch and then his attention is caught by the door handle being turned. He looks at the door but no one enters although the handle keeps being turned. Eventually he goes to the door and pulls it open*

RITA *is standing in the doorway, holding a small can of oil*

FRANK Oh.

RITA Hello. I was just oilin' it for y'. *(She comes into the room)* I knew you wouldn't get round to it. Y' can have that.

She gives the oil can to FRANK

FRANK Erm – thanks. *(He puts the can on the filing cabinet and then goes and sits in the swivel chair)*

Slightly amused, he watches her as she wanders round the room

RITA *(turning to him)* What y' lookin' at?

FRANK Don't you ever just walk into a room and sit down?

RITA Not when I've got the chair with its back to the door.

FRANK *(getting up)* Well – if it'd make you happier you take my chair.

RITA No. You're the teacher, you sit there.

FRANK But it doesn't matter where I sit. If you'd be happier with that chair then you sit there.

RITA Tch. Is that what y' call democracy at work? I don't wanna sit down anyway. I like walkin' around this room.

(After a pause) How d' y' make a room like this?

FRANK I didn't make it. I just moved in. The rest sort of happened.

RITA *(looking round)* Yeh. That's cos you've got taste. I'm gonna have a room like this one day. There's nothing phoney about it. Everything's in its right place. *(After a pause)* It's a mess. But it's a perfect mess. *(She wanders around)* It's like wherever you've put something down it's grown to fit there.

FRANK *(sitting down)* You mean that over the years it's acquired a certain patina.

RITA Do I?

FRANK I think so.

RITA Yeh. 'It's acquired a certain patina.' It's like something' from a romantic film, isn't it? 'Over the years your face has acquired a certain patina.'

FRANK *smiles*

RITA *(sniffing)* You've not been drinking, have y'?

FRANK No.

RITA Is that because of me, because of what I said last week?

FRANK *(laughing)* My God. You think you've reformed me?

RITA *(going to the window)* I don't wanna reform y'. Y' can do what y' like. *(Quickly)* I love that lawn down there. When it's summer do they sit on it?

FRANK *(going to the window)* Who?

RITA *(going back to the desk)* The ones who come here all the time. The proper students.

FRANK Yes. First glimmer of sun and they're all out there.

RITA Readin' an' studyin'?

FRANK Reading and studying? What do you think they are, human? Proper students don't read and study.

RITA Y' what?

FRANK A joke, a joke. Yes. They read and study, sometimes.

Pause. RITA *dumps her bag on the chair and then goes and hangs up her coat on the door*

RITA It looks the way I always imagined a public school to look, y' know a boardin' school. When I was a kid I always wanted to go to a boardin' school.

FRANK God forbid it; why?

RITA *(going to her chair at the desk)* I always thought they sounded great, schools like that, y' know with a tuck-shop an' a matron an' prep. An' a pair of kids called Jones minor an' Jones major. I told me mother once. *(She opens her bag and takes out the copy of 'Howards End', ring bound file, note-pad, ruler and pencil-case, placing them methodically on the desk in front of her)* She said I was off me cake.

FRANK *(with an exaggerated look at her)* What in the name of God is being off one's cake?

RITA Soft. Y' know, mental.

FRANK Aha. I must remember that. The next student to ask me if Isabel Archer was guilty of protestant masochism shall be told that one is obviously very off one's cake!

RITA Don't be soft. You can't say that.

FRANK Whyever not?

RITA You can't. If you do it, it's slummin' it. Comin' from you it'd sound dead affected, wouldn't it?

FRANK Dead affected?

RITA Yeh. You say that to your proper students they'll think you're off your – y' know …

FRANK Cake, yes. Erm – Rita, why didn't you ever become what you call a proper student?

RITA What? After goin' to the school I went to?

FRANK Was it bad?

RITA *starts sharpening the pencils one by one into perfect spikes, leaving the shavings on the desk*

RITA Nah, just normal, y' know; borin', ripped-up books, broken glass everywhere, knives an' fights. An' that was just in the staffroom. Nah, they tried their best I suppose, always tellin' us we stood more of a chance if we studied. But studyin' was just for the whimps, wasn't it? See, if I'd started takin' school seriously I would have had to become different from me mates, an' that's not allowed.

FRANK By whom?

RITA By your mates, by your family, by everyone. So y' never admit that school could be anythin' other than useless.

31

FRANK *passes her the ashtray but she ignores it and continues sharpening the pencils on to the table*

RITA Like what you've got to be into is music an' clothes an' lookin' for a feller, y' know the real qualities of life. Not that I went along with it so reluctantly. I mean, there was always somethin' in me head, tappin' away, telling' me I might have got it all wrong. But I'd just play another record or buy another dress an' stop worryin'. There's always somethin' to make you forget about it. So y' do, y' keep goin', tellin' yourself life's great. There's always another club to go to, a new feller to be chasin', a laugh an' a joke with the girls. Till, one day, y' own up to yourself an y' say, is this it? Is this the absolute maximum I can expect from this livin' lark? An' that's the big moment that one, that's the point when y' have to decide whether it's gonna be another change of dress or a change in yourself. An' it's really temptin' to go out an' get another dress y' know, it is. Cos it's easy, it doesn't cost anythin', it doesn't upset anyone around y'. Like cos they don't want y' to change.

FRANK But you – erm – you managed to resist another new dress?

RITA Can't y' tell? Look at the state of this; I haven't had a new dress in twelve months. An' I'm not gonna get one either, not till – till I pass me first exam. Then I'll get a proper dress, the sort of dress you'd only see on an educated woman, on the sort of woman who knows the difference between Jane Austen an' Tracy Austin. *(She finishes sharpening the last pencil, and arranges it in line with the others. She gathers the pencil shavings into her hand and chucks them in the waste-bin)* Let's start.

FRANK Now the piece you wrote for me on – what was it called …?

RITA *(getting out her cigarettes and lighter)* Rubyfruit Jungle.

FRANK Yes, it was – erm …

RITA Crap?

FRANK No. Erm – the thing is, it was an appreciation, a descriptive piece. What you have to learn is criticism.

RITA What's the difference? *(She lights a cigarette)*

FRANK Well. You must try to remember that criticism is purely objective. It should be approached almost as a science. It must be supported by reference to established literary critique. Criticism is never subjective and should not be confused with partisan interpretation. In criticism sentiment has no place. *(He picks up the copy of 'Howards End')* Tell me, what did you think of *Howards End*?

RITA It was crap.

FRANK What?

RITA I thought it was crap!

FRANK Crap? And who are you citing in support of your thesis, F. R. Leavis?

RITA No. Me!

FRANK What have I just said? 'Me' is subjective.

RITA Well it's what I think.

FRANK You think *Howards End* is crap? Well would you kindly tell me why you think it's quote, 'Crap', unquote.

RITA Yeh, I will tell y'. It's crap because the feller who wrote it was a louse. Because halfway through that book I couldn't go on readin' it because he, Mr Bleedin' E. M. Forster says, quote 'We are not concerned with the poor' unquote. That's why it's crap. An' that's why I didn't go on readin' it, that's why.

FRANK *(astounded)* Because he said we are not concerned with the poor?

RITA Yeh, that's it!

FRANK But he wasn't writing about the poor.

RITA When he wrote that book the conditions of the poor in this country were appalling. An' he's sayin' he couldn't care less. Mr E. M. Bleedin' Foster.

FRANK Forster.

RITA I don't care what his name was, he was sittin' up there in his ivory tower an' sayin' he couldn't care less.

FRANK *laughs*

RITA Don't laugh at me.

FRANK *(getting up)* But you cannot interpret E. M. Forster from a Marxist viewpoint.

RITA Why?

FRANK Look, before discussing this I said no subjectivity, no sentimentality.

RITA I wasn't bein' sentimental.

FRANK Of course you were. You stopped reading the book because you wanted Forster to concern himself with the poor. Literature can ignore the poor.

RITA Well, it's immoral.

FRANK *(wandering around)* Amoral. But you wanted to know. You see what sort of a mark you'd get if you approached Forster in this way during an examination?

RITA What sort?

FRANK Well, you might manage one or two per cent if the examiner was sympathetic to the one dubious quality your criticism displays.

RITA What's that?

FRANK Brevity.

RITA All right. But I hated that book. Can't we do somethin' else? Can't we do somethin' I like?

FRANK But the sort of stuff you like is not necessarily the sort of thing that will form the basis of your examination next Christmas. Now if you're going to pass any sort of exam you have to begin to discipline that mind of yours.

RITA Are you married?

FRANK *(moving back to the swivel chair)* It's – ogh …

RITA Are y'? What's y' wife like?

FRANK Is my wife at all relevant?

RITA What? You should know, you married her.

FRANK Well, she's not relevant. I haven't seen her for a long time. We split up. All right?

RITA I'm sorry.

FRANK Why are you sorry?

RITA I'm sorry for askin'. For bein' nosey.

FRANK (sitting in the swivel chair) The thing about Howards End is that …

RITA Why did y' split up?

FRANK (taking off his glasses and looking at her) Perhaps you'd like to take notes! When you have to answer a question on Forster you can treat the examiner to an essay called Frank's marriage!

RITA Oh go way. I'm only interested.

FRANK (leaning towards her; conspiratorially) We split up, Rita, because of poetry.

RITA Y' what?

FRANK One day my wife pointed out to me that for fifteen years my output as a poet had dealt exclusively with the period in which we – discovered each other.

RITA Are you a poet?

FRANK Was. And so, to give me something new to write about she left. A very noble woman my wife. She left me for the good of literature.

RITA An' what happened?

FRANK She was right. Her leaving was an enormous benefit to literature.

RITA What, y' wrote a load of good stuff?

FRANK No. I stopped writing altogether.

RITA (slightly puzzled) Are you takin' the piss?

FRANK gives a short laugh and leans back in his chair

FRANK No.

RITA People don't split up because of things like that. Because of literature.

FRANK Maybe you're right. But that's how I remember it.

RITA Were you a famous poet?

FRANK No. I sold a few books, all out of print now.

RITA Can I read some of your stuff?

FRANK You wouldn't like it.

RITA How d' y' know?

FRANK It's the sort of poetry you can't understand – unless you happen to have a detailed knowledge of the literary references.

RITA Oh. *(After a pause)* Do you live on y' own then?

FRANK Rita! Tch.

RITA I was only askin'.

FRANK I live with a girl. Ex student. She's very caring, very tolerant, admires me enormously and spends a great deal of time putting her head in the oven.

RITA Does she try an' do herself in?

FRANK Mm? No, she just likes to watch the ratatouille cook.

RITA The what?

FRANK Ratatouille. Though Julia has renamed it the 'stop-outs dish'. It can simmer in an oven for days. In our house it often has no choice.

RITA D' you stop out for days?

FRANK Occasionally. And that is the end of …

RITA Why do y'?

FRANK And that is the end of that.

RITA If y' were mine an' y' stopped out for days y' wouldn't get back in.

FRANK Ah, but Rita, if I was yours would I stop out for days?

RITA Don't y' like Julia?

FRANK I like her enormously; it's myself I'm not too fond of.

RITA Tch. Y' great …

FRANK A vote of confidence; thank you. But, I'm afraid, Rita, that you'll find there's less to me than meets the eye.

RITA See – look – y' can say dead clever things like that, can't y'? I wish I could talk like that. It's brilliant.

FRANK Staggering. Now look, *Howards ... (He swivels the chair round so that he faces away from* RITA**)**

RITA Oh ey ... leave that. I just like talkin' to y'. It's great. That's what they do wrong in schools y' know – *(she gets up and warms her legs by the fire)* – they get y' talkin' an' that, an y' all havin' a great time talkin' about somethin' an' the next thing they wanna do is turn it into a lesson. We was out with the teacher once, y' know outside school, an' I'm right at the back with these other kids an' I saw this fantastic bird, all coloured it was, like dead out of place round our way. I was just gonna shout an' tell Miss but this kid next to me said, 'Keep your mouth shut or she'll make us write an essay on it.'

FRANK *(sighing)* Yes, that's what we do, Rita; we call it education.

RITA Tch. Y'd think there was somethin' wrong with education to hear you talk.

FRANK Perhaps there is.

RITA So why are y' givin' me an education?

FRANK Because it's what you want, isn't it? What I'd actually like to do is take you by the hand and run out of this room forever.

RITA *(going back to her chair)* Tch – be serious ...

FRANK I am. Right now there's a thousand things I'd rather do than teach; most of them with you, young lady ...

RITA *(smiling gently)* Tch. Oh sod off ... You just like saying things like that. *(She sits down)*

FRANK Do I?

RITA Yeh. Y' know y' do.

FRANK Rita – why didn't you walk in here twenty years ago?

RITA Cos I don't think they would have accepted me at the age of six.

FRANK You know what I mean.

RITA I know. But it's not twenty years ago, Frank. It's now. You're there an' I'm here.

FRANK Yes. And you're here for an education. *(He waves his finger)* You must keep reminding me of that. Come on, Forster!

RITA Tch. Forget him.

FRANK Listen to me; you said that I was going to teach you. You want to learn. Well that, I'm afraid, means a lot of work. You've barely had a basic schooling, you've never passed an examination in your life. Possessing a hungry mind is not, in itself, a guarantee of success.

RITA All right. But I just don't like *Howards* bleedin' *End*.

FRANK Then go back to what you do like and stop wasting my time. You go out and buy yourself a new dress and I'll go to the pub.

RITA *(after a pause)* Is that you putting your foot down?

FRANK It is actually.

RITA Oh. Aren't you impressive when y' angry?

FRANK Forster!

RITA All right, all right, Forster. Does Forster's repeated use of the phrase 'only connect' suggest that he was really a frustrated electrician?

FRANK Rita.

RITA In considering Forster it helps if we examine the thirteen amp plug …

Black-out

RITA *goes out*

Notes for Act 1 Scenes 3 and 4

Rita is now well into her course and has begun to read more widely, though her essays still do not please Frank. We see evidence of her intelligence, however, in her response to what she has read. We learn, too, about her husband's opposition to what she is doing and about her own forcefully expressed opinions on the working-class world she inhabits.

What do you think?
Discussions and misunderstandings about culture play a large part in these two scenes. Frank tries to make clear to Rita the difference between 'pulp fiction' and 'literature' and she, in turn, is very scornful of working-class culture. As you read through the scenes think about:
- whether you agree with Rita's views
- what she has learned by the end of the two scenes.

Questions
Look for the answers to these questions and the details in the text which support your ideas.
1. What is wrong with Rita's essay on *Howards End* and the two she writes on *Peer Gynt*?
2. Why does Frank tell Rita the story of the theology student?
3. Why does he suggest Rita should take a course in politics?
4. Why do you think Rita says 'it makes me stronger coming here'?
5. Why do you think Willy Russell chooses *Howards End* as the first book Rita has to read on her course?

Further activity
By this stage in the play, we know quite a lot about both Rita and Frank. You can start to prepare a character log. For each of them, draw up a chart with four columns headed *Key Point*, *Comment*, *Quotation* and *Page*. In the first column, include such details as appearance, movement, what s/he says or does, what they say about each other and other people and so on. In the second column, jot down briefly what this tells you about each character and how s/he may be changing. Include an appropriate supporting quotation in column three and give a page reference in the fourth column so that you can check back at any time.

Scene 3

The lights come up on FRANK *working at his desk*

RITA *flounces into the room and goes to the desk*

RITA God, I've had enough of this. It's borin', that's what it is, bloody borin'. This Forster, honest to God he doesn't half get on my tits.

She dumps her bag on the chair and makes towards the hook by the door, by taking off her coat as she goes. She hangs the coat on the hook

FRANK Good. You must show me the evidence.

RITA Y' dirty sod.

FRANK *(Wagging his finger at her)* True, true … it's cutting down on the booze that's done it. Now. *(He waves a sheet of paper at her)* What's this?

RITA *(sitting by the desk)* It's a bleedin' piece of paper, isn't it?

FRANK It's your essay. Is it a joke? Is it?

RITA No. It's not a joke.

FRANK Rita, how the hell can you write an essay on E. M. Forster with almost total reference to Harold Robbins?

RITA Well? You said bring in other authors.

FRANK Tch.

RITA Don't go on at me. You said; y' said, 'Reference to other authors will impress the examiners'.

FRANK I said refer to other works but I don't think the examiner, God bless him, will have read, *(he consults the paper)* A Stone For Danny Fisher.

RITA Well, that's his hard luck, isn't it?

FRANK It'll be your hard luck when he fails your paper.

RITA Oh that's prime, isn't it? That's justice for y'. I get failed just cos I'm more well read than the friggin' examiner!

FRANK Devouring pulp fiction is not being well read.

RITA I thought reading was supposed to be good for one. *(She gets out her cigarettes)*

FRANK It is, but you've got to be selective. In your favour you do mention *Sons and Lovers* somewhere in here. When did you read that?

RITA This week. I read that an' the Harold Robbins an' this dead fantastic book, what was it called? Erm – ogh what was it? It sounded like somethin' dead perverted, it was by that English feller ...

FRANK Which English feller?

RITA You know, the one who was like Noël Coward – erm. Oh, I know – Somerset Maughan.

FRANK A perverted book by Somerset Maugham?

RITA No, it wasn't perverted it was great – the title sounds perverted ...

He starts to laugh

Don't laugh.

FRANK Do you mean *Of Human Bondage?*

RITA Yeh – that's it. Well it does sound perverted doesn't it?

FRANK Well! *(After a pause)* You read three novels this week?

RITA *(taking a cigarette from the pack)* Yeh. It was dead quiet in the shop.

FRANK And if I asked you to make a comparison between those books, what would you say?

RITA Well, they were all good in their own way.

FRANK But surely you can see the difference between the Harold Robbins and the other two.

RITA Apart from that one bein' American like?

FRANK Yes.

RITA Yeh. I mean the other two were sort of posher. But they're all books, aren't they?

FRANK Yes. Yes. But you seem to be under the impression that all books are literature.

RITA Aren't they?

FRANK No.

RITA Well – well how d' y' tell?

FRANK I – erm – erm – one's always known really.

RITA But how d' y' work it out if y' don't know? See that's what I've got to learn, isn't it? I'm dead ignorant y' know.

FRANK No. You're not ignorant. It's merely a question of becoming discerning in your choice of reading material.

RITA I've got no taste. Is that what you're saying?

FRANK No.

RITA It is. Don't worry. I won't get upset. I'm here to learn. My mind's full of junk, isn't it? It needs a good clearin' out. Right, that's it, I'll never read a Robbins novel again.

FRANK Read it, by all means read it. But don't mention it in an exam.

RITA Aha. You mean, it's all right to go out an' have a bit of slap an' tickle with the lads as long as you don't go home an tell your mum?

FRANK Erm – well yes, that's probably what I do mean.

Black-out

RITA *exits*

Scene 4

The lights come up on FRANK *who is standing by the window*

RITA *enters and shuts the door behind her, standing just inside the room*

FRANK *goes to his briefcase on the window-desk and starts looking for Rita's 'Peer Gynt' essay*

RITA I can't do it. Honest, I just can't understand what he's on about. *(She goes to her chair at the desk, dumps her bag and then goes and hangs up her coat)* He's got me licked, I don't know what he's on about, 'Only connect, only connect', it's just bleedin' borin'. It's no good, I just can't understand.

FRANK You will. You will.

RITA It's all right for you sayin' that. You know what it's about. *(She goes to her chair by the desk)* But I just can't figure it.

FRANK Do you think we could forget about Forster for a moment?

RITA With pleasure.

FRANK *takes the 'Peer Gynt' essay and stands over her for a moment. Then he perches on the corner of the desk* UP RIGHT

FRANK I want to talk about this that you sent me. *(He holds up a sheet of A4 paper)*

RITA That? Oh.

FRANK Yes. In response to the question, 'Suggest how you would resolve the staging difficulties inherent in a production of Ibsen's *Peer Gynt*', you have written, quote, 'Do it on the radio', unquote.

RITA Precisely.

FRANK Well?

RITA Well what?

FRANK Well I know it's probably quite naïve of me but I did think you might let me have a considered essay.

RITA *sits down by the desk and unpacks the student's pad, pencil case, ruler, copy of 'Peer Gynt' and eight reference books from her bag*

RITA That's all I could do in the time. We were dead busy in the shop this week.

FRANK You write your essays at work?

RITA Yeh.

FRANK Why?

RITA Denny get's dead narked if I work at home. He doesn't like me doin' this. I can't be bothered arguin' with him.

FRANK But you can't go on producing work as thin as this.

RITA Is it wrong?

FRANK No, it's not wrong, it's just …

RITA See, I know it's short. But I thought it was the right answer.

FRANK It's the basis for an argument, Rita, but one line is hardly an essay.

RITA I know, but I didn't have much time this week, so I sort of, y' know, encapsulated all me ideas in one line.

FRANK But it's not enough.

RITA Why not?

FRANK It just isn't.

RITA But that's bleedin' stupid, cos you say – you say, don't y' – that one line of exquisite poetry says more than a thousand pages of second-rate prose?

FRANK But you're not writing poetry. What I'm trying to make you see is that whoever was marking this would want more than, 'Do it on the radio'. *(He gets up and moves around to the other side of Rita's chair)* There is a way of answering examination questions that is expected. It's a sort of accepted ritual, it's a game, with rules. And you must observe those rules. *(He leans with one hand on the back of Rita's chair)* When I was at university there was a student taking his final theology exam. He walked into the examination hall, took out his pen and wrote 'God knows all the answers', then he handed in his paper and left.

RITA *(impressed)* Did he?

FRANK When his paper was returned to him, his professor had written on it, 'And God gives out the marks'.

RITA Did he fail?

FRANK *(breaking away slightly)* Of course he failed. You see a clever answer is not necessarily the correct answer.

RITA *(getting out her cigarettes)* I wasn't tryin' to be clever; I didn't have much time an' I …

FRANK All right, but look, you've got some time now. *(He leans on her chair, bending over her)* Just give it a quarter of an hour or so adding some considered argument to this: 'In attempting to resolve the staging difficulties in *Peer Gynt* I would present it on the radio because … ' and outline your reasons supporting them, as much as possible, with quotes from accepted authorities. All right?

RITA Yeh. All right *(She picks up the essay, pen, copy of 'Peer Gynt', eight reference books, sticks the cigarette in her mouth, and starts to move towards the window desk)*

FRANK Now, are you sure you understand?

RITA *stops and speaks over her shoulder with the cigarette still in her mouth*

RITA Yeh. What d' y' think I am, thick? *(She takes her usual chair and puts it in front of the window desk. She sits down and puts her belongings on the desk, moving Frank's briefcase out of the way)*

FRANK *moves the swivel chair to the* UP *end of his desk and settles down to marking essays*

RITA *leans back in the chair and tries to blow smoke-rings*

Y' know Peer Gynt? He was searchin' for the meaning of life wasn't he?

FRANK Erm – put at its briefest, yes.

RITA Yeh. *(She pauses)* I was doin' this woman's hair on Wednesday …

FRANK Tch …

RITA *(facing* FRANK*)* I'm gonna do this, don't worry. I'll do it. But I just wanna tell y'; I was doin' her hair an' I was dead bored with what the others in the shop were talkin' about. So I just said to this woman, I said, 'Do you know about *'Peer Gynt?'* She thought it was a new perm lotion. So I told her all about it, y' know the play. An' y' know somethin', she was dead interested, she was y' know.

FRANK Was she?

RITA Yeh. She said, 'I wish I could go off searchin' for the meanin' of life.' There's loads of them round by us who feel like that. Cos by us there is no meanin' to life. *(She thinks)* Frank, y' know culture, y' know the word culture? Well it doesn't just mean goin' to the opera an' that, does it?

FRANK No.

RITA It means a way of livin', doesn't it? Well we've got no culture.

FRANK Of course you have.

RITA What? Do you mean like that working-class culture thing?

FRANK Mm.

RITA Yeh. I've read about that. I've never seen it though.

FRANK Well, look around you.

RITA I do. But I don't see any, y' know, culture. I just see everyone pissed, or on the Valium, tryin' to get from one day to the next. Y' daren't say that round our way like, cos they're proud. They'll tell y' they've got culture as they sit there drinkin' their keg beer out of plastic glasses.

FRANK Yes, but there's nothing wrong with that, if they're content with it.

During the following FRANK's *attention is caught gradually and he stops marking and starts listening*

RITA But they're not. Cos there's no meanin'. They tell y' stories about the past, y' know, the war, or when they were

47

fightin' for food an' clothin' an' houses. Their eyes light up as they tell y', because there was some meanin' to it. But the thing is that now, I mean now that most of them have got some sort of house an' there's food an' money around, they know they're better off but, honest, they know they've got nothin' as well. There's like this sort of disease, but no one mentions it; everyone behaves as though it's normal, y' know inevitable that there's vandalism an' violence an' houses burnt out an' wrecked by the people they were built for. There's somethin' wrong. An' like the worst thing is that y' know the people who are supposed to like represent the people on our estate, y' know the *Daily Mirror* an' the *Sun,* an' ITV an' the Unions, what are they tellin' people to do? They just tell them to go out an' get more money, don't they? But they don't want more money; it's like me, isn't it? Y' know, buyin' new dresses all the time, isn't it? The Unions tell them to go out an' get more money an' ITV an' the papers tell them what to spend it on so the disease is always covered up.

FRANK *swivels round in his chair to face* RITA

FRANK *(after a pause)* Why didn't you take a course in politics?

RITA Politics? Go way, I hate politics. I'm just tellin' y' about round our way. I wanna be on this course findin' out. You know what I learn from you, about art an' literature, it feeds me, inside. I can get through the rest of the week if I know I've got comin' here to look forward to. Denny tried to stop me comin' tonight. He tried to get me to go out to the pub with him an' his mates. He hates me comin' here. It's like drug addicts, isn't it? They hate it when one of them tries to break away. It makes me stronger comin' here. That's what Denny's frightened of.

FRANK 'Only connect.'

RITA Oh, not friggin' Forster again.

FRANK 'Only connect.' You see what you've been doing?

RITA Just tellin' y' about home.

FRANK Yes, and connecting, your dresses/ITV and the *Daily Mirror.* Addicts/you and your husband.

RITA Ogh!

FRANK You see?

RITA An' – an' in that book – no one does connect.

FRANK Irony.

RITA Is that it? Is that all it means?

FRANK Yes.

RITA Why didn't y' just tell me, right from the start?

FRANK I could have told you; but you'll have a much better understanding of something if you discover it in your own terms.

RITA *(sincerely)* Aren't you clever?

FRANK Brilliant. Now. *Peer Gynt.*

RITA All right, all right, hold on. *(She opens a couple of books and starts writing)*

FRANK *continues his marking and does not notice as* RITA *finishes writing. She picks up her chair, essay, pen and books, and moves across in front of his desk. She replaces the chair by the desk and stands watching him*

FRANK *(looking up)* What?

RITA I've done it.

FRANK You've done it?

She hands him the essay

(Reading aloud) 'In attempting to resolve the staging difficulties in a production of Ibsen's *Peer Gynt* I would present it on the radio because as Ibsen himself says, he wrote the play as a play for voices, never intending it to go on in a theatre. If they had the radio in his day that's where he would have done it.'

He looks up as she beams him a satisfied smile
Black-out

Notes for Act 1 Scene 5

Rita's relationship with her husband has reached a crisis, but she is determined to continue with her course, no matter what it costs her. She tries, not very successfully, to find out more about Frank's past and his personal life. The end of the scene sees Rita intent on furthering her cultural education by going to the theatre for the first time.

What do you think?
The scene indirectly throws some light on Rita's and Frank's relationships with their partners. Naturally, as we only hear about Denny and Julia through what their partners say about them, these accounts might be rather biased. As you read this scene think about:
- whether you have any sympathy for Denny and Julia
- whether there are any similarities between Frank and Denny.

Questions
Look for the places in the text which support your answers to these questions:
1. What expressions does Rita use to emphasise how important the course is to her?
2. Why won't she go to the pub with Frank?
3. What do you think Frank means when he says that 'poets shouldn't believe in literature'?
4. Why is Frank so reluctant to go to see the production of *The Importance of Being Earnest*?
5. What words used by Frank indicate that he finds Rita attractive? Is he serious?

Further activity
Imagine that you are Denny, Rita's husband. Working with a partner, improvise a scene, perhaps in the pub, in which you talk to your best friend about the problems you are having with her. Try to bring out how you feel, basing what you say on the evidence in the play. You could also improvise a similar scene in which Julia and her friend discuss her problems with Frank. When you have finished your improvisations, you could use them as the basis for a piece of writing in which Denny justifies his actions in burning Rita's books.

Scene 5

As the lights come up FRANK *is sitting in the swivel chair and* RITA *stands by the filing cabinet*

FRANK What's wrong? *(After a pause)* You know this is getting to be a bit wearisome. When you come to this room you'll do anything except start work immediately. Couldn't you just come in prepared to start work? Where's your essay?

RITA *(staring out of the window)* I haven't got it.

FRANK You haven't done it?

RITA I said I haven't got it.

FRANK You've lost it?

RITA It's burnt.

FRANK Burnt?

RITA So are all the Chekhov books you lent me. Denny found out I was on the pill again; it was my fault, I left me prescription out. He burnt all me books.

FRANK Oh Christ!

RITA I'm sorry. I'll buy y' some more.

FRANK I wasn't referring to the books. Sod the books.

RITA Why can't he just let me get on with me learnin'? You'd think I was havin' a bloody affair the way he behaves.

FRANK And aren't you?

RITA *wanders* DOWN RIGHT *She fiddles with the library steps, smoothing the top step*

RITA *(looking at him)* No. What time have I got for an affair? I'm busy enough findin' meself, let alone findin' someone else. I don't want anyone else. I've begun to find me – an' it's great y' know, it is Frank. It might sound selfish but all I want for the time bein' is what I'm findin' inside me. I certainly don't wanna be rushin' off with some feller, cos

51

the first thing I'll have to do is forget about meself for the sake of him.

FRANK Perhaps, perhaps your husband thinks you're having an affair with me.

RITA Oh go way. You're me teacher. I've told him.

FRANK You've told him about me? What?

RITA (*sitting down*) I've – tch – I've tried to explain to him how you give me room to breathe. Y' just, like feed me without expectin' anythin' in return.

FRANK What did he say?

RITA He didn't. I was out for a while. When I come back he'd burnt me books an' papers, most of them. I said to him, y' soft get, even if I was havin' an affair there's no point burnin' me books. I'm not havin' it off with Anton Chekhov. He said, 'I wouldn't put it past you to shack up with a foreigner'.

FRANK (*after a pause*) What are you going to do?

RITA I'll order some new copies for y' an' do the essay again.

FRANK I mean about your husband.

RITA (*Standing up*) I've told him, I said, 'There's no point cryin' over spilt milk, most of the books are gone, but if you touch my *Peer Gynt* I'll kill y'.'

FRANK Tch. Be serious.

RITA I was!

FRANK Do you love him?

RITA (*after a pause*) I see him lookin' at me sometimes, an' I know what he's thinkin, I do y' know, he's wonderin' where the girl he married has gone to. He even brings me presents sometimes, hopin' that the presents'll make her come back. But she can't, because she's gone, an' I've taken her place.

FRANK Do you want to abandon this course?

RITA No. No!

FRANK When art and literature begin to take the place of life itself, perhaps it's time to …

RITA (*emphatically*) But its not takin' the place of life, it's providin' me with life itself. He wants to take life away from me; he wants me to stop rockin' the coffin, that's all. Comin' here, doin' this, it's given me more life then I've had in years, an' he should be able to see that. Well, if he doesn't want me when I'm alive I'm certainly not just gonna lie down an' die for him. I told him I'd only have a baby when I had choice. But he doesn't understand. He thinks we've got choice because we can go into a pub that sells eight different kinds of lager. He thinks we've got choice already: choice between Everton an' Liverpool, choosin' which washin' powder, choosin' between one lousy school an' the next, between lousy jobs or the dole, choosin' between Stork an' butter.

FRANK Yes. Well, perhaps your husband …

RITA No. I don't wanna talk about him. *(She comes to the front of the desk)* Why was Chekhov a comic genius?

FRANK Rita. Don't you think that for tonight we could give the class a miss?

RITA No. I wanna know. I've got to do this. He can burn me books an' me papers but if it's all in me head he can't touch it. It's like that with you, isn't it? You've got it all inside.

FRANK Let's leave it for tonight. Let's go to the pub and drink pots of Guinness and talk.

RITA I've got to do this, Frank. I've got to. I want to talk about Chekhov.

FRANK We really should talk about you and Denny, my dear.

RITA I don't want to.

FRANK *(after a pause)* All right. Chekhov.

RITA *goes to the* UP *end of the desk and stands between the chair and the desk*

FRANK 'C' for Chekhov.

He gets up and moves towards the bookcase, taking RITA'*s chair with him. He stands on the chair and begins rummaging on the top shelf, dropping some of the books on the floor.* RITA *turns to sit down and notices her chair has gone. She sees* FRANK *and watches him as he finds a bottle of whisky hidden behind some books. He gets down and takes the whisky to the small table*

We'll talk about Chekhov and pretend this is the pub.

RITA Why d' y' keep it stashed behind there?

FRANK *(pouring the drinks)* A little arrangement I have with my immediate employers. It's called discretion. They didn't tell me to stop drinking, they told me to stop displaying the signs.

RITA *(climbing on to the chair to replace the books)* Do you actually like drinking?

FRANK Oh yes. I love it. Absolutely no guilt at all about it.

RITA Know when you were a poet, Frank, did y' drink then?

FRANK Some. Not as much as now. *(He takes a drink)* You see, the great thing about the booze is that it makes one believe that under all the talk one is actually saying something.

RITA Why did you stop bein' a poet?

FRANK *(wagging his finger at her)* That is a pub question.

RITA Well. I thought we were pretendin' this was the pub. *(She gets down from the chair)*

FRANK In which we would discuss Chekhov.

RITA Well he's second on the bill. You're on first. Go on, why did y' stop?

FRANK I didn't stop, so much as realize I never was. I'd simply got it wrong, Rita. *(After a pause)* Instead of creating poetry I spent – oh – years and years trying to create literature. You see?

RITA *(replacing her chair UP of the desk)* Well I thought that's what poets did.

FRANK What? *(He gives RITA her drink)*

RITA Y' know, make literature. *(She perches on the small table)*

FRANK *(shaking his head)* Poets shouldn't believe in literature.

RITA *(puzzled)* I don't understand that

FRANK You will. You will.

RITA Sometimes I wonder if I'll ever understand any of it. It's like startin' all over again, y' know with a different language.

Know I read that Chekhov play an' I thought it was dead sad, it was tragic; people committin' suicide an' that Constantin kid's tryin' to produce his masterpiece an' they're all laughin' at him? It's tragic. Then I read the blurb on it an' everyone's goin' on about Chekhov bein' a comic genius.

FRANK Well, it's not comedy like – erm – well it's not stand-up comedy. Have you ever seen Chekhov in the theatre?

RITA No. Does he go?

FRANK Have you ever been to the theatre?

RITA No.

FRANK You should go.

RITA *(standing up)* Hey! Why don't we go tonight?

FRANK Me? Go to the theatre? God no, I hate the theatre.

RITA Why the hell are y' sendin' me?

FRANK Because you want to know.

RITA *(packing her things into her bag)* Well, you come with me.

FRANK And how would I explain that to Julia?

RITA Just tell her y' comin' to the theatre with me.

FRANK 'Julia, I shall not be in for dinner as I am going to the theatre with ravishing Rita.'

RITA Oh sod off.

FRANK I'm being quite serious.

RITA Would she really be jealous?

FRANK If she knew I was at the theatre with an irresistible thing like you? Rita, it would be deaf and dumb breakfasts for a week.

RITA Why?

FRANK Why not?

RITA I dunno – I just thought …

FRANK *(pouring himself another drink)* Rita, ludicrous as it may seem to you, even a woman who possesses an M.A. is not above common jealousy.

RITA Well, what's she got to be jealous of me for? I'm not gonna try an' rape y' in the middle of *The Seagull*.

FRANK What an awful pity. You could have made theatre exciting for me again.

RITA Come on, Frank. Come with me. Y' never tell the truth you, do y'?

FRANK What d' y' mean?

RITA Y' don't; y' like evade it with jokes an' that, don't y'? Come on, come to the theatre with me. We'll have a laugh …

FRANK Will we?

RITA Yeh. C'mon we'll ring Julia. *(She goes to the telephone and picks up the receiver)*

FRANK What!

RITA C'mon, what's your number?

FRANK *(taking the receiver from her and replacing it)* We will not ring Julia. Anyway Julia's out tonight.

RITA So what will you do, spend the night in the pub?

FRANK Yes.

RITA Come with me, Frank, y'll have a better time than y' will in the pub.

FRANK Will I?

RITA Course y' will. *(She goes and gets both coats from the hook by the door, comes back and throws her coat over the back of the chair)*

FRANK *(putting down his mug on the bookcase)* What is it you want to see?

RITA *helps* FRANK *into his coat*

RITA *The Importance of Bein' Thingy* …

FRANK But *The Importance* isn't playing at the moment …

RITA It is – I passed the church hall on the bus an' there was a poster …

FRANK *breaks loose, turns to her and throws off his coat*

FRANK *(aghast)* An amateur production?

RITA What?

FRANK Are you suggesting I miss a night at the pub to watch *The Importance* played by amateurs in a church hall?

RITA *picks his coat up and puts it round his shoulders*

RITA Yeh. It doesn't matter who's doin' it, does it? It's the same play, isn't it?

FRANK Possibly, Rita … *(He switches off the desk lamp)*

RITA *(putting on her coat and picking up her bag)* Well come on – hurry up – I'm dead excited. I've never seen a live play before.

FRANK *goes round switching off the electric fire and desk lamp and then picks up his briefcase*

FRANK And there's no guarantee you'll see a 'live' play tonight.

RITA Why? Just cos they're amateurs? Y've gorra give them a chance. They have to learn somewhere. An' they might be good.

FRANK *(doubtfully)* Yes …

RITA Oh y' an awful snob, aren't y'?

FRANK *(smiling acknowledgement)* All right – come on.

They go towards the door

RITA Have you seen it before?

FRANK Of course.

RITA Well, don't go tellin' me what happens will y'? Don't go spoilin' it for me.

FRANK *switches off the light switch. Black-out*

FRANK *and* RITA *exit*

Notes for Act 1 Scene 6

Rita continues to develop. She has been to see a professionally produced Shakespeare play for the first time and enthusiastically gives her opinions on it. The play is *Macbeth* and Frank explains to her what 'tragedy' means. Rita's cultural horizons are expanding and she proposes a visit to an art gallery. Frank invites Rita to his home for a dinner party.

What do you think?

Earlier in the play, Frank had spoken about 'comedy' to Rita. In this scene, he shows her that what is commonly thought of as 'tragic' is not the same as 'tragedy'. He stresses that one of the important features of a tragedy is the inevitability of the fate that awaits the hero, because of a flaw in his character. As you read the play, consider:

- whether there is any connection between Frank's definition of tragedy and his own fate
- what warnings about her own fate Rita is given during the play.

Questions

Read the scene carefully to find the answers to these questions:

1. What words does Rita use to express her enthusiasm for *Macbeth*? Could she use these words in an essay?
2. What is the difference, according to Frank, between 'tragic' and 'a tragedy'?
3. Why does Willy Russell have Rita and Frank offer each other an apple and a can of soft drink?
4. Why does Rita say, 'All them out there, they know about that sort of thing don't they'?
5. Why does Frank invite Rita to dinner?

Further activity

In the theatre, costume, lighting and stage design are important in contributing to the overall effect of a play. Imagine that you have been asked to design a set for *Educating Rita*. You'll have to look closely at the text to see exactly what is needed. Produce a detailed drawing or sketch plan of your proposed set and then write notes for the director, explaining the reasons for your design.

Scene 6

The lights come up

FRANK *enters carrying a briefcase and a pile of essays. He goes to the filing cabinet, takes his lecture notes from the briefcase and puts them in a drawer. He takes the sandwiches and apple from his briefcase and puts them on his desk and then goes to the window desk and dumps the essays and briefcase. He switches on the radio and then sits in the swivel chair. He opens the packet of sandwiches, takes a bite and then picks up a book and starts reading*

RITA *bursts through the door out of breath*

FRANK What are you doing here? *(He looks at his watch)* It's Thursday, you …

RITA *(moving over to the desk; quickly)* I know I shouldn't be here, it's me dinner hour, but listen, I've gorra tell someone, have y' got a few minutes, can y' spare …?

FRANK *(alarmed)* My God, what is it?

RITA I had to come an' tell y', Frank, last night, I went to the theatre! A proper one, a professional theatre.

Frank gets up and switches off the radio and then returns to the swivel chair

FRANK *(sighing)* For God's sake, you had me worried, I thought it was something serious.

RITA No, listen, it was. I went out an' got me ticket, it was Shakespeare, I thought it was gonna be dead borin' …

FRANK Then why did you go in the first place?

RITA I wanted to find out. But listen, it wasn't borin', it was bleedin' great, honest, ogh, it done me in, it was fantastic. I'm gonna do an essay on it.

FRANK *(smiling)* Come on, which one was it?

RITA *moves* UP RIGHT CENTRE

59

RITA ' ... Out, out, brief candle!

Life's but a walking shadow, a poor player

That struts and frets his hour upon the stage

And then is heard no more. It is a tale

Told by an idiot, full of sound and fury

Signifying nothing.'

FRANK (deliberately) Ah, *Romeo and Juliet*.

RITA (moving towards FRANK) Tch. Frank! Be serious. I learnt that today from the book. (*She produces a copy of 'Macbeth'*) Look, I went out an' bought the book. Isn't it great? What I couldn't get over is how excitin' it was.

FRANK *puts his feet up on the desk*

RITA Wasn't his wife a cow, eh? An' that fantastic bit where he meets Macduff an' he thinks he's all invincible. I was on the edge of me seat at that bit. I wanted to shout out an' tell Macbeth, warn him.

FRANK You didn't, did you?

RITA Nah. Y' can't do that in a theatre, can y'? It was dead good. It was like a thriller.

FRANK Yes. You'll have to go and see more.

RITA I'm goin' to. Macbeth's a tragedy, isn't it?

FRANK *nods*

RITA Right.

RITA *smiles at* FRANK *and he smiles back at her* Well I just – I just had to tell someone who'd understand.

FRANK I'm honoured that you chose me.

RITA (*moving towards the door*) Well, I better get back. I've left a customer with a perm lotion. If I don't get a move on there'll be another tragedy.

FRANK No. There won't be a tragedy.

RITA There will, y' know. I know this woman; she's dead fussy. If her perm doesn't come out right there'll be blood an' guts everywhere.

FRANK Which might be quite tragic –

He throws her the apple from his desk which she catches

– but it won't be a tragedy.

RITA What?

FRANK Well – erm – look; the tragedy of the drama has nothing to do with the sort of tragic event you're talking about. Macbeth is flawed by his ambition – yes?

RITA *(going and sitting in the chair by the desk)* Yeh. Go on.

(She starts to eat the apple)

FRANK Erm – it's that flaw which forces him to take the inevitable steps towards his own doom. You see?

RITA *offers him the can of soft drink. He takes it and looks at it*

FRANK *(putting the can down on the desk)* No thanks. Whereas, Rita, a woman's hair being reduced to an inch of stubble, or – or the sort of thing you read in the paper that's reported as being tragic, 'Man Killed By Falling Tree', is not a tragedy.

RITA It is for the poor sod under the tree.

FRANK Yes, it's tragic, absolutely tragic. But it's not a tragedy in the way that *Macbeth* is a tragedy. Tragedy in dramatic terms is inevitable, pre-ordained. Look, now, even without ever having heard the story of *Macbeth* you wanted to shout out, to warn him and prevent him going on, didn't you? But you wouldn't have been able to stop him would you?

RITA No.

FRANK Why?

RITA They would have thrown me out the theatre.

FRANK But what I mean is that your warning would have been ignored. He's warned in the play. But he can't go back. He still treads the path to doom. But the poor old fellow under the tree hasn't arrived there by following any inevitable steps has he?

RITA No.

FRANK There's no particular flaw in his character that has dictated his end. If he'd been warned of the consequences of standing beneath that particular tree he wouldn't have done it, would he? Understand.

RITA So – so Macbeth brings it on himself?

FRANK Yes. You see he goes blindly on and on and with every step he's spinning one more piece of thread which will eventually make up the network of his own tragedy. Do you see?

RITA I think so. I'm not used to thinkin' like this.

FRANK It's quite easy, Rita.

RITA It is for you. I just thought it was a dead excitin' story. But the way you tell it you make me see all sorts of things in it. *(After a pause)* It's fun, tragedy, isn't it? *(She goes over to the window)* All them out there, they know all about that sort of thing don't they?

FRANK Look, how about a proper lunch?

RITA Lunch? *(She leaps up, grabs the copy of 'Macbeth', the can of drink and the apple and goes to the door)* Christ – me customer. She only wanted a demi-wave – she'll come out looking like a friggin' muppet *(She comes back to the table)* Ey' Frank, listen – I was thinkin' of goin' to the art gallery tomorrow. It's me half-day off. D' y' wanna come with me?

FRANK *(smiling)* All right.

RITA *goes to the door*

FRANK *(looking at her)* And – look, what are you doing on Saturday?

RITA I work.

FRANK Well, when you finish work.

RITA Dunno.

FRANK I want you to come over to the house.

RITA Why?

FRANK Julia's organized a few people to come round for dinner.

RITA An' y' want me to come? Why?

FRANK Why do you think?

RITA I dunno.

FRANK Because you might enjoy it.

RITA Oh.

FRANK Will you come?

RITA If y' want.

FRANK What do you want?

RITA All right. I'll come.

FRANK Will you bring Denny?

RITA I don't know if he'll come.

FRANK Well ask him.

RITA *(puzzled)* All right.

FRANK What's wrong?

RITA What shall I wear?

Black-out

RITA *goes out*

Notes for Act 1 Scenes 7 and 8

These two scenes form an effective climax to the first act. In them, we learn about a number of important decisions that Rita makes which will determine her future. Having been briefly tempted back to her old way of life, Rita resists and makes the momentous decision to leave her husband. The new Rita who has emerged during the course of this act cannot go back: she must continue her education.

What do you think?

The end of the first act of a two-act play is an appropriate time to reflect on what has happened to the characters so far. As there are only two characters who appear on stage throughout *Educating Rita*, this should make it easier for you. As you read these scenes, think about

- what changes, if any, have occurred in Rita and Frank and how their attitudes to each other have changed
- the advantages and disadvantages of a play that has only two characters always in the same setting.

Questions

Remember to base your answers to these questions on evidence from the text.

1. Why didn't Rita go to Frank's dinner party?

2. Why do you think her mother's words 'we could sing better songs than those' had such an effect on Rita?

3. What does Frank mean when he says that Rita's essay on *Macbeth* is 'worthless' and 'wonderful'?

4. Why does the act end with 'an' we start again'?

Further activity

The beginning of each scene is important in establishing the mood and the feelings of the characters even before a word is uttered. Draw up a chart with four columns headed *Scene, Rita, Frank* and *Comments*. Put the number of the scene in the first column, in the second and third what each character is doing before the conversation begins and how s/he enters the room, and in the last column comment on what these reveal about Frank and Rita's moods and feelings.

Scene 7

The lights come up on FRANK *who is sitting in the armchair listening to the radio*

RITA *enters, goes straight to the desk and slings her bag on the back of her chair*

She sits in the chair and unpacks the note-pad and pencil-case from her bag. She opens the pad and takes out the pencil-sharpener and pencils and arranges them as before. FRANK *gets up, switches off the radio, goes to the swivel chair and sits*

FRANK Now I don't mind; two empty seats at the dinner table means more of the vino for me. But Julia – Julia is the stage-manager type. If we're having eight people to dinner she expects to see eight. She likes order – probably why she took me on – it gives her a lot of practice –

RITA *starts sharpening her pencils*

FRANK – and having to cope with six instead of eight was extremely hard on Julia. I'm not saying that I needed any sort of apology; you don't turn up that's up to you, but …

RITA I did apologize.

FRANK 'Sorry couldn't come', scribbled on the back of your essay and thrust through the letter box? Rita, that's hardly an apology.

RITA What does the word 'sorry' mean if it's not an apology? When I told Denny we were goin' to yours he went mad. We had a big fight about it.

FRANK I'm sorry. I didn't realize. But look, couldn't you have explained? Couldn't you have said that was the reason?

RITA No. Cos that wasn't the reason. I told Denny if he wasn't gonna go I'd go on me own. An' I tried to. All day Saturday, all day in the shop I was thinkin' what to wear. I got back, an' I tried on five different dresses. They all looked bleedin' awful. An' all the time I'm trying to think of things I can say, what I can talk about. An' I can't remember anythin'. It's all jumbled up in me head. I can't remember if it's Wilde who's witty an' Shaw who was Shavian or who the hell wrote *Howards End*.

FRANK Ogh God!

RITA Then I got the wrong bus to your house. It took me ages to find it. Then I walked up your drive, an' I saw y' all through the window, y' were sippin' drinks an' talkin' an laughin'. An' I couldn't come in.

FRANK Of course you could.

RITA I couldn't. I'd bought the wrong sort of wine. When I was in the off licence I knew I was buyin' the wrong stuff. But I didn't know which was the right wine.

FRANK Rita for Christ's sake; I wanted *you* to come along. You weren't expected to dress up or buy wine.

RITA *(holding all the pencils and pens in her hands and playing with them)* If you go out to dinner don't you dress up? Don't you take wine?

FRANK Yes, but …

RITA Well?

FRANK Well what?

RITA Well you wouldn't take sweet sparkling wine, would y'?

FRANK Does it matter what I do? It wouldn't have mattered if you'd walked in with a bottle of Spanish plonk.

RITA It was Spanish.

FRANK Why couldn't you relax? *(He gets up and goes behind* RITA's *chair, then leans on the back of it)* It wasn't a fancy dress party. You could have come as yourself. Don't you realize how people would have seen you if you'd just – just breezed in? Mm? They would have seen someone who's funny, delightful, charming …

RITA *(angrily)* But I don't wanna be charming and delightful:

funny. What's funny? I don't wanna be funny. I wanna talk seriously with the rest of you, I don't wanna spend the night takin' the piss, comin' on with the funnies because that's the only way I can get into the conversation. I didn't want to come to your house just to play the court jester.

FRANK You weren't being asked to play that role. I just – just wanted you to be yourself.

RITA But I don't want to be myself. Me? What's me? Some stupid woman who gives us all a laugh because she thinks she can learn, because she thinks that one day she'll be like the rest of them, talking seriously, confidently, with knowledge, livin' a civilized life. Well, she can't be like that really but bring her in because she's good for a laugh!

FRANK If you believe that that's why you were invited, to be laughed at, then you can get out, now. (*He goes to his desk and grabs the pile of essays, taking them to the window desk. He stands with his back to* RITA *and starts pushing the essays into his briefcase*) You were invited because I wished to have your company and if you can't believe that then I suggest you stop visiting me and start visiting an analyst who can cope with paranoia.

RITA I'm all right with you, here in this room; but when I saw those people you were with I couldn't come in. I would have seized up. Because I'm a freak. I can't talk to the people I live with any more. An' I can't talk to the likes of them on Saturday, or them out there, because I can't learn the language. I'm a half-caste. I went back to the pub where Denny was, an' me mother, an' our Sandra, an' her mates. I'd decided I wasn't comin' here again.

FRANK *turns to face her*

RITA I went into the pub an' they were singin', all of them singin' some song they'd learnt from the juke-box. An' I stood in that pub an' thought, just what the frig am I trying to do? Why don't I just pack it in an' stay with them, an' join in the singin'?

FRANK And why don't you?

RITA *(angrily)* You think I can, don't you? Just because you pass a pub doorway an' hear the singin' you think we're all O. K., that we're all survivin', with the spirit intact. Well I did join in with the singin', I didn't ask any questions, I just went along with it.

But when I looked round me mother had stopped singin', an' she was cryin', but no one could get it out of her why she was cryin'. Everyone just said she was pissed an' we should get her home. So we did, an' on the way I asked her why. I said, 'Why are y' cryin', Mother?' She said, 'Because – because we could sing better songs than those.' Ten minutes later, Denny had her laughing and singing again, pretending she hadn't said it. But she had. And that's why I came back. And that's why I'm staying.

Black-out

RITA *goes out*

helen g troj

Menelayos got in with the house

Scene 8

The lights come up on FRANK *seated in the swivel chair at the desk reading* RITA *'s 'Macbeth' essay*
RITA *enters slowly, carrying a suitcase*

FRANK *(without looking up)* One second.

She puts down the suitcase RIGHT CENTRE *and wanders slowly* RIGHT *with her back to* FRANK

(He closes the essay he has been reading, sighs and removes his glasses) Your essay. *(He sees the suitcase)* What's that?

RITA It's me case.

FRANK Where are you going?

RITA Me mother's.

FRANK What's wrong? *(After a pause)* Rita!

RITA I got home from work, he'd packed me case. He said either I stop comin' here an' come off the pill or I could get out altogether.

FRANK Tch.

RITA It was an ultimatum. I explained to him. I didn't get narked or anythin'. I just explained to him how I had to do this. He said it's warped me. He said I'd betrayed him. I suppose I have.

FRANK Why have you?

RITA I have. I know he's right. But I couldn't betray meself. *(After a pause)* He says there's a time for education. An' it's not when y' twenty-six an' married.

FRANK *gets up and goes towards* RITA *who still faces away from him*

FRANK *(after a pause)* Where are you going to stay?

RITA I phoned me mother; she said I could go there for a week. Then I'll get a flat. *(She starts to cry)* I'm sorry, it's just …

FRANK *takes hold of her and tries to guide her to the chair* DOWN RIGHT

69

FRANK Look, come on, sit down.

RITA *(breaking away from him)* It's all right – I'll be O. K. Just give me a minute. *(She dries her eyes)* What was me *Macbeth* essay like?

FRANK Oh sod *Macbeth*.

RITA Why?

FRANK Rita!

RITA No, come on, come on, I want y' to tell me what y' thought about it.

FRANK In the circumstances …

RITA *(going and hanging her bag on the back of the swivel chair)* It doesn't matter, it doesn't; in the circumstances I need to go on, to talk about it an' do it. What was it like? I told y' it was no good. Is it really useless?

FRANK *sits in the chair* DOWN RIGHT

FRANK *(sighing)* I – I really don't know what to say.

RITA Well try an' think of somethin'. Go on, I don't mind if y' tell me it was rubbish. I don't want pity, Frank. Was it rubbish?

FRANK No, no. It's not rubbish. It's a totally honest, passionate account of your reaction to a play. It's an unashamedly emotional statement about a certain experience.

RITA Sentimental?

FRANK No. It's too honest for that. It's almost – erm – moving. But in terms of what you're asking me to teach you of passing exams ... Oh, God, you see, I don't …

RITA Say it, go on, say it!

FRANK In those terms it's worthless. It shouldn't be, but it is; in it's own terms it's – it's wonderful.

RITA *(confronting him across the desk)* It's worthless! You said. An' if it's worthless you've got to tell me because I wanna write essays like those on there. *(She points to the essays on the desk)* I wanna know, an' pass exams like they do.

FRANK But if you're going to write this sort of stuff you're going to have to change.

RITA All right. Tell me how to do it.

FRANK *(getting up)* But I don't know if I want to tell you, Rita, I don't know that I want to teach you. *(He moves towards the desk)* What you already have is valuable.

RITA Valuable? What's valuable? The only thing I value is here, comin' here once a week.

FRANK But, don't you see, if you're going to write this sort of thing – (he *indicates the pile of essays*) – to pass examinations, you're going to have to suppress, perhaps even abandon your uniqueness. I'm going to have to change you.

RITA But, don't you realize, I want to change! Listen, is this your way of tellin' me that I can't do it? That I'm no good?

FRANK It's not that at …

RITA If that's what you're trying' to tell me I'll go now …

FRANK *turns away from her*

FRANK *(moving away from the desk)* No no no. Of course you're good enough.

RITA See I know it's difficult for y' with someone like me. But you've just gorra keep tellin' me an' then I'll start to take it in; y' see, with me you've got to he dead firm. You won't hurt me feelings y' know. If I do somethin' that's crap, I don't want pity, you just tell me, that's crap. *(She picks up the essay)* Here, it's crap. *(She rips it up)* Right. So we dump that in the bin, *(She does so)* an' we start again.

Notes for Act 2 Scene 1

We quickly realise, at the start of this new act, that significant changes have taken place in Rita's life since we last saw her. We do not see these happening, of course, but we do see and hear the results. She has been to Summer School and now lives in a flat with a friend, but it is the changes in her character and attitude that are perhaps the most startling.

What do you think?
The time that she spent at Summer School has had a major impact on Rita and we can see the effects of this in the scene, not only in the way she dresses but also in her attitude towards Frank. As you read the scene, think carefully about:
- the changes, both positive and negative, that have occurred in Rita
- Frank's responses to these changes.

Questions
Don't forget to pay careful attention to the text as you answer these questions:
1. How does Willy Russell indicate that time has passed between the end of Act 1 and the beginning of Act 2?
2. Why did Rita buy Frank a pen?
3. Frank addresses Rita as 'my dear' at one point. What does this tell us about his attitude towards her here?
4. What is the significance of the fact that the window 'won't bleedin' budge'?
5. Why do you think the scene ends with the words 'you don't do Blake without doing innocence and experience, do y'?'

Further activity
Imagine that this encounter with Rita has prompted Frank to start writing again. Write either the poem or the diary or journal entry in which he explores his feelings and reactions to the changes he has seen in Rita and her new attitude towards him. You'll have to keep checking on what he says in this scene (and others) to make sure you remain true to his character.

Act 2 Scene 1

When the curtain rises FRANK *is sitting at his desk typing poetry. He pauses, stubs out a cigarette, takes a sip from the mug at his side, looks at his watch and then continues typing*

RITA *bursts through the door. She is dressed in new, second-hand clothes*

RITA Frank! *(She twirls on the spot to show off her new clothes)*

FRANK *(smiling)* And what is this vision, returning from the city? *(He gets up and moves towards* RITA*)* Welcome back.

RITA Frank, it was fantastic.

She takes off her shawl and gives it to FRANK *who hangs it on the hook by the door.* RITA *goes to the desk*

(Putting down her bag on the desk) Honest, it was – ogh!

FRANK What are you talking about, London or summer school?

RITA Both. A crowd of us stuck together all week. We had a great time: dead late every night, we stayed up talkin', we went all round London, got drunk, went to the theatres, bought all sorts of second-hand gear in the markets ... Ogh, it was ...

FRANK So you won't have had time to do any actual work there?

RITA Work? We never stopped. Lashin' us with it they were; another essay, lash, do it again, lash.

FRANK *moves towards the desk*

RITA Another lecture, smack. It was dead good though. *(She goes and perches on the bookcase* UP RIGHT*)*

FRANK *sits in the swivel chair, facing her*

RITA Y' know at first I was dead scared. I didn't know anyone. I was gonna come home. But the first afternoon I was standin' in this library, y' know lookin' at the books, pretendin' I was dead clever. Anyway, this tutor come up to me, he looked at the book in me hand an' he said, 'Ah, are you fond of Ferlinghetti?' It was right on the tip of me tongue to say, 'Only when it's served with Parmesan cheese', but, Frank, I didn't. I held it back an' I heard meself sayin', 'Actually, I'm not too familiar with the American poets'. Frank, you woulda been dead proud of me. He started talkin' to me about the American poets – we sat around for ages – an' he wasn't even one of my official tutors, y' know. We had to go to this big hall for a lecture, there must have been two thousand of us in there. After he'd finished his lecture this professor asked if anyone had a question, an' Frank, I stood up! *(She stands)* Honest to God, I stood up, an' everyone's lookin' at me. I don't know what possessed me, I was gonna sit down again, but two thousand people had seen me stand up, so I did it, I asked him the question.

There is a pause and FRANK *waits*

FRANK Well?

RITA Well what?

FRANK What was the question?

RITA Oh, I dunno, I forget now, cos after that I was askin' questions all week, y' couldn't keep me down. I think that first question was about Chekhov; cos y' know I'm dead familiar with Chekhov now.

He smiles. RITA *moves to the chair by the desk and sits.* FRANK *swivels round to face her*

Hey, what was France like? Go on, tell us all about it.

FRANK There isn't a lot to tell.

RITA Ah go on, tell me about it; I've never been abroad. Tell me what it was like.

FRANK Well – it was rather hot … *(He offers her a Gauloise)*

RITA No, ta, I've packed it in. Did y' drink?

FRANK Ah – a little. *(He puts the cigarettes on the table)*

RITA Tch. Did y' write?

FRANK A little.

RITA Will y' show it to me?

74

FRANK Perhaps … One day, perhaps.

RITA So y' wrote a bit an' y' drank a bit? Is that all?

FRANK *(in a matter of fact tone)* Julia left me.

RITA What?

FRANK Yes. But not because of the obvious, oh no – it had nothing whatsoever to do with the ratatouille. It was actually caused by something called *oeufs en cocotte.*

RITA What?

FRANK Eggs, my dear, eggs. Nature in her wisdom cursed me with a dislike for the egg be it cocotte, Florentine, Benedict or plain hard-boiled. Julia insisted that nature was wrong. I defended nature and Julia left.

RITA Because of eggs?

FRANK Well – let's say that it began with eggs. *(He packs away the typewriter)* Anyway, that's most of what happened in France. Anyway, the holiday's over, you're back, even Julia's back.

RITA Is she? Is it all right?

FRANK *(putting the typewriter on the window desk and the sheets of poetry in the top left drawer)* Perfect. I get the feeling we shall stay together forever; or until she discovers *oeufs à la crécy.*

RITA *Oeufs* à *la crécy?* Does that mean eggs? Trish was goin' on about those; is that all it is, eggs?

FRANK Trish?

RITA Trish, me flatmate, Trish. God is it that long since I've seen y', Frank? She moved into the flat with me just before I went to summer school.

FRANK Ah. Is she a good flatmate?

RITA She's great. Y' know she's dead classy. Y' know like, she's got taste, y' know like you, Frank, she's just got it. Everything in the flat's dead unpretentious, just books an' plants everywhere. D' y' know somethin', Frank? I'm havin' the time of me life; I am y' know. I even feel – *(moving to the window)* – I feel young, you know like them down there.

FRANK My dear, twenty-six is hardly old.

RITA I know that; but I mean, I feel young like them … I can be young. *(She goes to her bag)* Oh listen – *(she puts the bag on the desk and rummages in it, producing* a box) – I bought y' a present back from London – it isn't much but I thought …

She gives him a small box

Here.

FRANK *puts on his glasses, gets the scissors out of the pot on the desk, cuts the string and opens the box to reveal an expensive pen*

RITA See what it says – it's engraved.

FRANK *(reading)* 'Must only be used for poetry. By strictest order – Rita' … *(He looks up at her)*

RITA I thought it'd be like a gentle hint.

FRANK Gentle?

RITA Every time y' try an' write a letter or a note with that pen, it won't work; you'll read that inscription an' it'll make you feel dead guilty – cos y' not writing poetry. *(She smiles at him)*

FRANK *(getting up and pecking her on the cheek)* Thank you – Rita. *(He sits down again)*

RITA It's a pleasure. Come on. *(She claps her hands)* What are we doin' this term? Let's do a dead good poet. Come on, let's go an' have the tutorial down there.

FRANK *(appalled)* Down where?

RITA *(getting her bag)* Down there – on the grass – come on.

FRANK On the grass? Nobody sits out there at this time of year.

RITA They do – *(looking out of the* window) – there's some of them out there now.

FRANK Well they'll have wet bums.

RITA What's a wet bum. You can sit on a bench. *(She tries to pull him to his feet)* Come on.

FRANK *(remaining sitting)* Rita, I absolutely protest.

RITA Why?

FRANK Like Dracula, I have an aversion to sunlight.

RITA Tch. *(She sighs)* All right. *(She goes to the window)* Let's open a window.

FRANK If you must open a window then go on, open it. *(He swivels round to watch her)*

RITA *(Struggling to open the window)* It won't bleedin' budge.

FRANK I'm not surprised, my dear. It hasn't been opened for generations.

RITA *(abandoning it)* Tch. Y' need air in here, Frank. The room needs airing. *(She goes and opens the door)*

FRANK This room does not need air, thank you very much.

RITA Course it does. A room is like a plant.

FRANK A room is like a plant?

RITA Yeh, it needs air. *(She goes to her chair by the desk and sits)*

FRANK And water, too, presumably? *(He gets up and closes the door)* If you're going to make an analogy why don't we take it the whole way? Let's get a watering-can and water the carpet; bring in two tons of soil and a bag of fertilizer. Maybe we could take cuttings and germinate other little rooms.

RITA Go way, you're mental, you are.

FRANK You said it, distinctly, you said, a room is like a plant.

RITA Well!

There is a pause

FRANK Well what?

RITA Well any analogy will break down eventually.

FRANK Yes. And some will break down sooner than others. *(He smiles, goes to the bookcase UP LEFT and begins searching among the books)* Look, come on … A great poet you wanted – well – we have one on the course …

RITA *sits on the desk watching* FRANK

FRANK I was going to introduce you to him earlier. *(As he rummages a book falls to one side revealing a bottle of whisky which has been hidden behind it)* Now – where is he …?

RITA *goes over and picks up the whisky bottle from the shelf*

RITA Are you still on this stuff?

FRANK Did I ever say I wasn't?

RITA *(putting the bottle down and moving away)* No. But …

FRANK But what?

RITA Why d' y' do it when y've got so much goin' for y', Frank?

FRANK It is indeed because I have 'so much goin' for me' that I do it. Life is such a rich and frantic whirl that I need the drink to help me step delicately through it.

RITA It'll kill y', Frank.

FRANK Rita, I thought you weren't interested in reforming me.

RITA I'm not. It's just …

FRANK What?

RITA Just that I thought you'd started reforming yourself.

FRANK Under your influence?

She shrugs

(He stops searching and turns to face her) Yes. But Rita – if I repent and reform, what do I do when your influence is no longer here? What do I do when, in appalling sobriety, I watch you walk away and disappear, my influence gone forever?

RITA Who says I'm gonna disappear?

FRANK Oh you will, Rita. You've got to. *(He turns back to the shelves)*

RITA Why have I got to? This course could go on for years. An' when I've got through this one I might even get into the proper university here.

FRANK And we'll all live happily ever after? Your going is as inevitable as – as …

RITA *Macbeth?*

FRANK *(smiling)* As tragedy, yes: but it will not be a tragedy, because I shall be glad to see you go.

RITA Tch. Thank you very much. *(After a pause)* Will y' really?

FRANK Be glad to see you go? Well I certainly don't want to see you stay in a room like this for the rest of your life. Now. *(He continues searching for the book)*

RITA *(after a pause)* You can be a real misery sometimes, can't y'? I was dead happy a minute ago an' then you start an' make me feel like I'm having a bad night in a mortuary.

FRANK *finds the book he has been looking for and moves towards* RITA *with it*

FRANK Well here's something to cheer you up – here's our 'dead good' poet – Blake.

RITA Blake? William Blake?

FRANK The man himself. *You* will understand Blake; they over complicate him, Rita, but you will understand – you'll love the man.

RITA I know.

FRANK What? *(He opens the book)* Look – look – read this … *(He hands her the book and then goes and sits in the swivel chair)*

RITA *looks at the poem on the page indicated and then looks at* FRANK

RITA *(reciting from memory)*

'O Rose, thou art sick!
The invisible worm
That flies in the night,
In the howling storm,

Has found out thy bed
Of crimson joy:
And his dark secret love
Does thy life destroy.'

FRANK You know it!

RITA *(laughing)* Yeh. *(She tosses the book on the desk and perches on the* UP LEFT *bookcase)* We did him at summer school.

FRANK Blake at summer school? You weren't supposed to do Blake at summer school, were you?

RITA Nah. We had this lecturer though, he was a real Blake freak. He was on about it every day. Everythin' he said, honest, everything was related to Blake – he couldn't get his dinner in the refectory without relating it to Blake – Blake and Chips. He was good though. On the last day we brought him a present, an' on it we put that poem, y' know, 'The Sick Rose'. But we changed it about a bit; it was – erm –

'O Rose, thou aren't sick
Just mangled and dead
Since the rotten gardener
Pruned off thy head.'

We thought he might be narked but he wasn't, he loved it.

He said – what was it ...? He said, 'Parody is merely a compliment masquerading as humour.'

FRANK *(getting up and replacing the book on the shelf)* So you've already done Blake? You covered all the *Songs of Innocence and Experience?*

RITA Of course; you don't do Blake without doing innocence and experience, do y'?

FRANK No. Of course. *(He goes and sits in the swivel chair)*
Black-out

RITA *picks up her bag and shawl and exits*

Notes for Act 2 Scenes 2 and 3

These two scenes show us further developments in Rita's character. She is now able to discuss literature confidently with the students she meets on the lawn and this confidence is further revealed in her argument with Frank about her interpretation of one of Blake's poems. Frank, in his turn, is somewhat taken aback by these changes in Rita and what appears to be her independence of mind.

What do you think?
When you have read these two scenes, you will see that Frank finds it difficult to cope with the 'new' Rita. Of course, as her teacher, he is partly responsible for what has happened, because teachers are expected to develop their pupils' potential. Consider carefully these issues raised in the scenes:

- whether the new, more educated Rita is wiser than the old
- what Frank's feelings are towards Rita.

Questions
1. Why does Rita change her way of speaking?
2. How have her views of students changed?
3. Why do you think Frank gets so very drunk at this particular point in the play?
4. What is the significance of Frank's definition of *assonance* as 'getting the rhyme wrong'?
5. What are Frank's criticisms of Rita's essay and how does she defend herself against them?

Further activity
A play communicates its meaning to an audience not just through the words that the characters speak but also, amongst other things, through the costumes that they wear. Design the costumes that you think Frank and Rita should wear during the play. Remember that costumes signal the personalities of their wearers and any changes in them that occur as the play proceeds. The designs need not be elaborate drawings – sketches will be adequate. Explain your reasons for your designs in a short note to the play's director.

Scene 2

The lights come up on FRANK *who is sitting at his desk marking an essay. Occasionally he makes a tutting sound and scribbles something. There is a knock at the door*

FRANK Come in.

RITA *enters, closes the door, goes to the desk and dumps her bag on it. She takes her chair and places it next to* FRANK *and sits down*

RITA *(talking in a peculiar voice)* Hello, Frank.

FRANK *(without looking up)* Hello. Rita, you're late.

RITA I know, Frank. I'm terribly sorry. It was unavoidable.

FRANK *(looking up)* Was it really? What's wrong with your voice?

RITA Nothing is wrong with it, Frank. I have merely decided to talk properly. As Trish says there is not a lot of point in discussing beautiful literature in an ugly voice.

FRANK You haven't got an ugly voice; at least you *didn't* have. Talk properly.

RITA I am talking properly. I have to practise constantly, in everyday situations.

FRANK You mean you're going to talk like that for the rest of this tutorial?

RITA Trish says that no matter how difficult I may find it I must persevere.

FRANK Well will you kindly tell Trish that I am not giving a tutorial to a Dalek?

RITA I am not a Dalek.

FRANK *(appealingly)* Rita, stop it!

RITA But Frank, I have to persevere in order that I shall.

FRANK Rita! Just be yourself.

RITA *(reverting to her normal voice)* I am being myself. *(She gets up and moves the chair back to its usual place)*

FRANK What's that?

RITA What?

FRANK On your back.

RITA *(reaching up)* Oh – it's grass.

FRANK Grass?

RITA Yeh, I got here early today. I started talking to some students down on the lawn. *(She sits in her usual chair)*

FRANK You were talking to students – down there?

RITA *(laughing)* Don't sound so surprised. I can talk now y' know, Frank.

FRANK I'm not surprised. Well! You used to be quite wary of them didn't you?

RITA God knows why. For students they don't half come out with some rubbish y' know.

FRANK You're telling me?

RITA I only got talking to them in the first place because as I was walking past I heard one of them sayin' as a novel he preferred *Lady Chatterley* to *Sons and Lovers*. I thought, I can keep walkin' and ignore it, or I can put him straight. So I put him straight. I walked over an' said, 'Excuse me but I couldn't help overhearin' the rubbish you were spoutin' about Lawrence'. Shoulda seen the faces on them, Frank. I said tryin' to compare *Chatterley* with *Sons and Lovers* is like tryin' to compare sparkling wine with champagne. The next thing is there's this heated discussion, with me right in the middle of it.

FRANK I thought you said the student claimed to 'prefer' *Chatterley,* as a novel.

RITA He did.

FRANK So he wasn't actually suggesting that it was superior.

RITA Not at first – but then he did. He walked right into it …

FRANK And so you finished him off, did you, Rita?

RITA Frank, he was askin' for it. He was an idiot. His argument just crumbled. It wasn't just me – everyone else agreed with me.

FRANK *returns to reading the essay*

RITA There was this really mad one with them; I've only been talkin' to them for five minutes and he's inviting me to go abroad with them all. They're all goin' to the South of France in the Christmas holidays, slummin' it.

FRANK You can't go.

RITA What?

FRANK You can't go – you've got your exams.

RITA My exams are before Christmas.

FRANK Well – you've got your results to wait for ...

RITA Tch. I couldn't go anyway.

FRANK Why? *(He looks at her)*

RITA It's all right for them. They *can* just jump into a bleedin' van an' go away. But I can't.

He returns to the essay

Tiger they call him, he's the mad one. His real name's Tyson but they call him Tiger.

FRANK *(looking up)* Is there any point me going on with this? *(He points to the essay)*

RITA What?

FRANK Is there much point in working towards an examination if you're going to fall in love and set off for the South of ...

RITA *(shocked)* What! Fall in love? With who? My God, Frank, I've just been talkin' to some students. I've heard of match-making but this is ridiculous.

FRANK All right, but please stop burbling on about Mr Tyson.

RITA I haven't been burbling on.

He returns to the essay

What's it like?

FRANK Oh – it – erm – wouldn't look out of place with these. *(He places it on top of a pile of other essays on his desk)*

RITA Honest?

FRANK Dead honest.

Black-out

FRANK *exits*

85

Scene 3

The lights come up on RITA *who is sitting in the armchair by the window, reading a heavy tome. There is the sound of muffled oaths from behind the door*

FRANK *enters carrying his briefcase. He is very drunk*

FRANK Sod them – no, fuck them! Fuck them, eh, Rita? *(He goes to the desk)*

RITA Who?

FRANK You'd tell them wouldn't you? You'd tell them where to get off. *(He gets a bottle of whisky from his briefcase)*

RITA Tell who, Frank?

FRANK Yes – students – students reported me! *(He goes to the bookcase* UP RIGHT *and puts the whisky on the shelf)* Me! Complained – you know something? They complained and it was the best lecture I've ever given.

RITA Were you pissed?

FRANK Pissed? I was glorious! Fell off the rostrum twice. *(He comes round to the front of his desk)*

RITA Will they sack you?

FRANK *(lying flat on the floor)* The sack? God no; that would involve making a decision. Pissed is all right. To get the sack it'd have to be rape on a grand scale; and not just the students either.

RITA *gets up and moves across to look at him*

FRANK That would only amount to a slight misdemeanour. For dismissal it'd have to be nothing less than buggering the bursar … They suggested a sabbatical for a year or ten … Europe – or America … I suggested that Australia might be more apt – the allusion was lost on them …

RITA Tch. Frank, you're mad.

FRANK Completely off my cake. I know.

RITA Even if y' don't think about yourself, what about the students?

FRANK *What* about the students?

RITA Well it's hardly fair on them if their lecturer's so pissed that he's falling off the rostrum. *(She goes to her chair by the desk and replaces the book in her bag)*

FRANK I might have fallen off, my dear, but I went down talking – and came up talking – never missed a syllable – what have they got to complain about?

RITA Maybe they did it for your own good.

FRANK Or maybe they did it because they're a crowd of mealy-mouthed pricks who wouldn't know a poet if you beat them about the head with one. *(He half-sits up)* 'Assonance' – I said to them – 'Assonance means getting the rhyme wrong ...' *(He collapses back on to the floor again)* They looked at me as though I'd desecrated Wordsworth's tomb.

RITA Look, Frank, we'll talk about the Blake essay next week, eh?

FRANK Where are you going? We've got a tutorial. *(He gets up and staggers towards her)*

RITA Frank, you're not in any fit state for a tutorial. I'll leave it with y' an' we can talk about it next week, eh?

FRANK No – no – you must stay – erm ... Watch this – sober? *(He takes a huge breath and pulls himself together)* Sober! Come on ...

He takes hold of RITA *and pushes her round the desk and sits her in the swivel chair*

You can't go. I want to talk to you about this. *(He gets her essay and shows it to her)* Rita, what's this?

RITA Is there something wrong with it?

FRANK It's just, look, this passage about 'The Blossom' you seem to assume that the poem is about sexuality.

RITA It is!

FRANK Is it?

87

RITA Well it's certainly a like richer poem, isn't it? If it's interpreted in that way.

FRANK Richer? Why richer? We discussed it. The poem is a simple, uncomplicated piece about blossom, as if seen from a child's point of view.

RITA *(shrugging)* In one sense. But it's like, like the poem about the rose, isn't it? It becomes a more rewarding poem when you see that it works on a number of levels.

FRANK Rita, 'The Blossom' is a simply uncomplicated ...

RITA Yeh, that's what you say, Frank; but Trish and me and some others were talkin' the other night, about Blake, an' what came out of our discussion was that apart from the simple surface value of Blake's poetry there's always a like erm – erm –

FRANK Well? Go on ...

RITA *(managing to)* – a like vein. Of concealed meaning. I mean if that poem's only about the blossom then its not much of a poem is it?

FRANK So? You think it gains from being interpreted in this way?

RITA *(slightly defiantly)* Is me essay wrong then, Frank?

FRANK It's not – not wrong. But I don't like it.

RITA You're being subjective.

FRANK *(half laughing)* Yes – yes I suppose I am. *(He goes slowly to the chair* UP CENTRE *of the desk and sits down heavily)*

RITA If it was in an exam what sort of mark would it get?

FRANK A good one.

RITA Well what the hell are you sayin' then?

FRANK *(shrugging)* What I'm saying is that it's up to the minute, quite acceptable, trendy stuff about Blake; but there's nothing of you in there.

RITA Or maybe Frank, y' mean there's nothing of your views in there.

FRANK *(after a pause)* Maybe that is what I mean?

RITA But when I first came to you, Frank, you didn't give me any views. You let me find my own.

FRANK *(gently)* And your views I still value. But, Rita, these aren't your views.

RITA But you told me not to have a view. You told me to be objective, to consult recognized authorities. Well that's what I've done; I've talked to other people, read other books an' after consultin' a wide variety of opinion I came up with those conclusions.

He looks at her

FRANK *(after a pause)* Yes. All right.

RITA *(rattled)* Look, Frank, I don't have to go along one hundred per cent with your views on Blake y' know. I can have a mind of my own can't I?

FRANK I sincerely hope so, my dear.

RITA And what's that supposed to mean?

FRANK It means – it means be careful.

RITA *jumps up and moves in towards* FRANK

RITA *(angrily)* What d' y' mean be careful? I can look after myself. Just cos I'm learnin', just cos I can do it now an' read what I wanna read an' understand without havin' to come runnin' to you every five minutes y' start tellin' me to be careful. *(She paces about)*

FRANK Because – because *I* care for you – I want you to care for yourself.

RITA Tch. *(She goes right up to* FRANK. *After a pause)* I – I care for you, Frank … But you've got to – to leave me alone a bit. I'm not an idiot now, Frank – I don't need you to hold me hand as much … I can – I can do things on me own more now … And I am careful. I know what I'm doin'. Just don't – don't keep treatin' me as though I'm the same as when I first walked in here. I understand now, Frank; I know the difference between – between – Somerset Maughan an' Harold Robbins. An' you're still treating me as though I'm hung up on *Rubyfruit Jungle. (She goes to the swivel chair and sits)* Just … You understand, don't you Frank?

FRANK Entirely, my dear.

RITA I'm sorry.

FRANK Not at all. *(After a pause)* I got around to reading it you know, *Rubyfruit Jungle.* It's excellent.

RITA *(laughing)* Oh go way, Frank. Of its type it's quite interesting. But it's hardly excellence.

Black-out

RITA *exits*

Notes for Act 2 Scenes 4 and 5

In a sense, these two scenes represent the crisis in the relationship between Frank and Rita. The cause of the conflict between them is Rita's response to Frank's own poetry which he has given her to criticise. In their discussion, whilst it is clear that he dislikes what Rita has become, she accuses him of not being able to accept that she has changed for the better since he first met her.

What do you think?
In her attack on him, Rita accuses Frank of being like a father who is unable to accept that his daughter has grown up. There may be some truth in the accusation, but is it the entire truth? Willy Russell has so skilfully created the two characters that we cannot only understand both of them but sympathise with how they feel. As you read these two scenes, think about:
- the nature of Frank's feelings towards Rita
- which of the two you have most sympathy for.

Questions
Think carefully about the answers to these questions, basing your answer on evidence from the text.
1. Why did Rita give up her hairdressing job?
2. Why do you think Frank gives her his own poetry to criticise? Why is he so scathing about her response to it?
3. Do you think Rita 'can do without' Frank?
4. What is the significance of Rita changing her name?
5. What point is Frank making when he suggests other names she could call herself?

Further activity
Imagine that you have been put in charge of the publicity for a production of *Educating Rita*. Your first task is to design an attractive poster for the production and the second is to write a press release to be sent to local newspapers and radio stations. Both should indicate something about the nature of the play and encourage people to come and see it, but remember not to give too much away about how the plot develops.

Scene 4

The lights come up on FRANK *sitting in the swivel chair*
RITA *enters and goes to the desk*

RITA Frank ...
He looks at his watch
I know I'm late ... I'm sorry.
He gets up and moves away
Am I too late? We were talkin'. I didn't notice the time.

FRANK Talking?

RITA Yeh. If it'll go in my favour we were talking about Shakespeare.

FRANK Yes ... I'm sure you were.

RITA Am I too late then? All right. I'll be on time next week. I promise.

FRANK Rita. Don't go.

RITA No – honestly, Frank – I know I've wasted your time. I'll see y' next week, eh?

FRANK Rita! Sit down!

RITA *goes to her usual chair and sits*

FRANK *(Going to the side of her)* When you were so late I phoned the shop.

RITA Which shop?

FRANK The hairdresser's shop. Where you work. Or, I should say, worked.

RITA I haven't worked there for a long time. I work in a bistro now.

FRANK You didn't tell me.

RITA Didn't I? I thought I did. I was telling someone.

FRANK It wasn't me.

RITA Oh. Sorry. *(After a pause)* What's wrong?

FRANK *(after a pause)* It struck me that there was a time when you told me everything.

RITA I thought I had told you.

FRANK No. Like a drink?

RITA Who cares if I've left hairdressin' to work in a bistro?

FRANK I care. *(He goes* up right *to the bookshelves and takes a bottle from an eye-level shelf)* You don't want a drink? Mind if I do?

RITA But why do you care about details like that? It's just boring, insignificant detail.

FRANK *(getting a mug from the small table)* Oh. Is it?

RITA That's why I couldn't stand being in a hairdresser's any longer; boring irrelevant detail all the time, on and on … Well I'm sorry but I've had enough of that. I don't wanna talk about irrelevant rubbish anymore.

FRANK And what do you talk about in your bistro? Cheers.

RITA Everything.

FRANK Everything?

RITA Yeh.

FRANK Ah.

RITA We talk about what's important, Frank, and we leave out the boring details for those who want them.

FRANK Is Mr Tyson one of your customers?

RITA A lot of students come in; he's one of them. You're not gonna give me another warning are y', Frank?

FRANK Would it do any good?

RITA Look, for your information I do find Tiger fascinatin', like I find a lot of the people I mix with fascinating; they're young, and they're passionate about things that matter. They're not trapped – they're too young for that. And I like to be with them.

FRANK *(moving* DOWN RIGHT *of the desk and keeping his back to her)* Perhaps – perhaps you don't want to waste your time coming here anymore?

RITA Don't be stupid. I'm sorry I was late. *(After a pause she gets up)* Look, Frank, I've got to go. I'm meeting Trish at seven. We're going to see a production of *The Seagull*.

FRANK Yes. *(He turns to face her)* Well. When Chekhov calls …

RITA Tch.

FRANK You can hardly bear to spend a moment here can you?

RITA *(moving towards him a little)* That isn't true. It's just that I've got to go to the theatre.

FRANK And last week you didn't turn up at all. Just a phone call to say you had to cancel.

RITA It's just that – that there's so many things happening now. It's harder.

FRANK As I said, Rita, if you want to stop com –

RITA *(going right up to him)* For God's sake, I don't want to stop coming here. I've got to come here. What about my exam?

FRANK Oh I wouldn't worry about that. You'd sail through it anyway. You really don't have to put in the odd appearance out of sentimentality; *(he moves round to the other side of the desk)* I'd rather you spared me that.

FRANK *goes to drink*

RITA If you could stop pouring that junk down your throat in the hope that it'll make you feel like a poet you might be able to talk about things that matter instead of where I do or don't work; an' then it might be worth comin' here.

FRANK Are you capable of recognizing what does or does not matter, Rita?

RITA I understand literary criticism, Frank. When I come here that's what we're supposed to be dealing with.

FRANK You want literary criticism? *(He looks at her for a moment and then goes to the top drawer of his desk and takes out two slim volumes and some typewritten sheets of poetry and hands them to her)* I want an essay on that lot by next week.

RITA What is it?

FRANK No sentimentality, no subjectivity. Just pure criticism. A critical assessment of a lesser known English poet. Me.

Black-out

RITA *exits*

Scene 5

The lights come up on FRANK *sitting in a chair by the window desk with a mug in his hand and a bottle of whisky on the desk in front of him listening to the radio. There is a knock at the door*

FRANK Come in.

RITA *enters and goes to the swivel chair behind Frank's desk*

FRANK *(Getting up and switching off the radio)* What the – what the hell are you doing here? I'm not seeing you till next week.

RITA Are you sober? Are you?

FRANK If you mean am I still this side of reasonable comprehension, then yes.

RITA *(going and standing next to him)* Because I want you to hear this when you're sober. *(She produces his poems)* These are brilliant. Frank, you've got to start writing again. *(She goes to the swivel chair and sits)* This is brilliant. They're witty. They're profound. Full of style.

FRANK *(going to the small table and putting down his mug)* Ah … tell me again, and again …

RITA They are, Frank. It isn't only me who thinks so. Me an' Trish sat up last night and read them. She agrees with me. Why did you stop writing? Why did you stop when you can produce work like this? We stayed up most of the night, just talking about it. At first we just saw it as contemporary poetry in its own right, you know, as somethin' particular to this century but look, Frank, what makes it more – more … What did Trish say – ? More resonant than – purely contemporary poetry in that you can see in it a direct line through to nineteenth-century traditions of – of like wit an' classical allusion.

FRANK *(going to the chair* UP *of the desk and standing by the side of it)* Er – that's erm – that's marvellous, Rita. How fortunate I

96

didn't let you see it earlier. Just think if I'd let you see it when you first came here.

RITA I know ... I wouldn't have understood it, Frank.

FRANK You would have thrown it across the room and dismissed it as a heap of shit, wouldn't you?

RITA *(laughing)* I know ... But I couldn't have understood it then, Frank, because I wouldn't have been able to recognize and understand the allusions.

FRANK Oh I've done a fine job on you, haven't I.

RITA It's true, Frank. I can see now.

FRANK You know, Rita, I think – I think that like you I shall change my name; from now on I shall insist upon being known as Mary, Mary Shelley – do you understand that allusion, Rita?

RITA What?

FRANK She wrote a little Gothic number called *Frankenstein.*

RITA So?

FRANK This – *(picking up his poetry and moving round to* RITA*)* – this clever, pyrotechnical pile of self-conscious allusion is worthless, talentless, shit and could be recognized as such by anyone with a shred of common sense. It's the sort of thing that gives publishing a bad name. Wit? You'll find more wit in the telephone book, and, probably, more insight. Its one advantage over the telephone directory is that it's easier to rip. *(He rips the poems up and throws the pieces on to the desk)* It is pretentious, characterless and without style.

RITA It's not.

FRANK Oh, I don't expect you to believe me, Rita; you recognize the hallmark of literature now, don't you? *(In a final gesture he throws a handful of the ripped pieces into the air and then goes to the chair* DOWN RIGHT *and sits)* Why don't you just go away? I don't think I can bear it any longer.

RITA Can't bear what, Frank?

FRANK You, my dear – you ...

RITA I'll tell you what you can't bear, Mr Self-Pitying Piss

Artist; what you can't bear is that I am educated now. What's up, Frank, don't y' like me now that the little girl's grown up, now that y' can no longer bounce me on daddy's knee an' watch me stare back in wide-eyed wonder at everything he has to say? I'm educated, I've got what you have an' y' don't like it because you'd rather see me as the peasant I once was; you're like the rest of them – you like to keep your natives thick, because that way they still look charming and delightful. I don't need you. *(She gets up and picking up her bag moves away from the desk in the direction of the door)* I've got a room full of books. I know what clothes to wear, what wine to buy, what plays to see, what papers and books to read. I can do without you.

FRANK Is that all you wanted. Have you come all this way for so very, very little?

RITA Oh it's little to you, isn't it? It's little to you who squanders every opportunity and mocks and takes it for granted.

FRANK Found a culture have you, Rita? Found a better song to sing have you? No – you've found a different song, that's all – and on your lips it's shrill and hollow and tuneless. Oh, Rita, Rita …

RITA Rita? *(She laughs)* Rita? Nobody calls me Rita but you. I dropped that pretentious crap as soon as I saw it for what it was. You stupid … Nobody calls me Rita.

FRANK What is it now then? Virginia?

RITA *exits*

FRANK Or Charlotte? Or Jane? Or Emily?

Black-out

Notes for Act 2 Scenes 6 and 7

The final scenes of the play show us both Frank and Rita about to embark on new stages of their lives. Frank is preparing to leave for Australia, having upset the university authorities once too often, whilst Rita, having successfully passed her exams, is facing a number of choices about the direction her life is to take. The importance of this, however, is that Rita is now able to take charge of her own life and to make decisions for herself.

What do you think?

Clearly, given the title of the play, one of its most important themes is education and, in particular, the education of Rita. As you read the final scene and think about the play as a whole, consider:

- what Rita has learned during the course of the play
- whether 'Educating Frank' might have been an alternative title.

Questions

1. Why do you think Willy Russell needed to include Act 2 Scene 6?
2. What does Trish's attempted suicide teach Rita?
3. How have her views of students changed since the beginning of the play?
4. Why does Frank give Rita a dress at this particular moment in the play?
5. Why do you think Willy Russell chose to end the play with Rita cutting Frank's hair?

Further activity

Many universities include in their prospectuses not only information about the courses you can take there, but also accounts of what it is like to be a student at that particular institution. The Open University is obviously rather different in that it caters for adults who are returning to study and living at home, but it still feels such accounts would be very helpful to new and prospective students. Imagine that Rita had been asked to contribute to this prospectus. Write her account of life as a student. Try to include information about the difficulties she faced, the teaching methods and work she encountered and whether she felt the course had benefited her.

Scene 6

The lights come up on FRANK *talking into the telephone. He is leaning against the bookshelf*

FRANK Yes … I think she works there … Rita White … No, no. Sorry … erm. What is it? … Susan White? No? … Thank you … Thanks …

The lights fade to black-out to denote the passing of some time and then come up on FRANK *sitting at his desk with his back to the audience. He is drunk and talking on the telephone*

Yes … Erm … Trish is it? … Erm, yes I'm a friend of Rita's … Rita … I'm sorry Susan … yes … could you just say that – erm – I've … it's – erm – Frank here … her tutor … Yes … well could you tell her that I have – erm – I've entered her for her examination … Yes you see she doesn't know the details … time and where the exam is being held … Could you tell her to call in? … Please … Yes … Thank you.

The lights fade to black-out

Scene 7

The lights come up

RITA *enters and shuts the door. She is wrapped in a large winter coat. She lights a cigarette and moves across to the filing cabinet and places a Christmas card with the others already there. She throws the envelope in the waste-bin and opens the door revealing* FRANK *with a couple of tea-chests either side of him. He is taken aback at seeing her and then he gathers himself and, picking up one of the chests, enters the room.* RITA *goes out to the corridor and brings in the other chest.*

FRANK *gets the chair from the* UP *end of his desk and places it by the* UP LEFT *bookcase. He stands on it and begins taking down the books from the shelves and putting them into the chests.* RITA *watches him but he continues as if she is not there*

RITA Merry Christmas, Frank. Have they sacked y'?

FRANK Not quite.

RITA Well, why y' – packing your books away?

FRANK Australia. *(After a pause)* Some weeks ago – made rather a night of it.

RITA Did y' bugger the bursar?

FRANK Metaphorically. And as it was metaphorical the sentence was reduced from the sack to two years in Australia. Hardly a reduction in sentence really – but …

RITA What y' gonna do?

FRANK *Bon voyage.*

RITA She's not goin' with y'?

FRANK *shakes his head.* RITA *begins helping him take down the books from the shelves and putting them in the chests*

RITA What y' gonna do?

FRANK What do you think I'll do? Aussie? It's a paradise for the likes of me.

102

RITA Tch. Come on, Frank …

FRANK It is. Didn't you know the Australians named their favourite drink after a literary figure? Forster's Lager they call it. Of course they get the spelling wrong – rather like you once did!

RITA Be serious.

FRANK For God's sake, why did you come back here?

RITA I came to tell you you're a good teacher. *(After a pause)* Thanks for enterin' me for the exam.

FRANK That's all right. I know how much it had come to mean to you.

RITA *perches on the small table while* FRANK *continues to take books from the upper shelves*

RITA You didn't want me to take it, did y'? Eh? You woulda loved it if I'd written, 'Frank knows all the answers', across me paper, wouldn't y'? I nearly did an' all. When the invigilator said, 'Begin', I turned over me paper with the rest of them, and while they were all scribbling away against the clock, I just sat there, lookin' at the first question. Y' know what it was, Frank? 'Suggest ways in which one might cope with some of the staging difficulties in a production of *Peer Gynt*.'

FRANK *gets down, sits on the chair and continues to pack the books*

FRANK Well, you should have had no trouble with that.

RITA I did though. I just sat lookin' at the paper an thinkin' about what you'd said. I tried to ignore it, to pretend that you were wrong. You think you gave me nothing; did nothing for me. You think I just ended up with a load of quotes an' empty phrases; an' I did. But that wasn't your doin'. I was so hungry. I wanted it all so much that I didn't want it to be questioned. I told y' I was stupid. It's like Trish, y' know me flatmate, I thought she was so cool an' together – I came home the other night an' she'd tried to top herself. Magic, isn't it? She spends half her life eatin' wholefoods an' health foods to make her live longer, an' the other half tryin' to kill herself. *(After a pause)* I sat lookin' at the question, an' thinkin' about it all. Then I picked up me pen an' started.

FRANK And you wrote, 'Do it on the radio'?

RITA I could have done. An' you'd have been proud of me if I'd done that an' rushed back to tell you – wouldn't y'? But I chose not to. I had a choice. I did the exam.

FRANK I know. A good pass as well.

RITA Yeh. An' it might be worthless in the end. But I had a choice. I chose, me. Because of what you'd given me I had a choice. I wanted to come back an' tell y' that. That y' a good teacher.

FRANK (stopping working and looking at her) You know erm – I hear very good things about Australia. Things are just beginning there. The thing is, why don't you – come as well? It'd be good for us to leave a place that's just finishing for one that's just beginning.

RITA Isn't that called jumpin' a sinkin' ship?

FRANK So what? Do you really think there's any chance of us keeping it afloat?

She looks at him and then at the shelves

RITA (seeing the empty whisky bottles) 'Ey, Frank, if there was threepence back on each of those bottles you could buy Australia.

FRANK (smiling) You're being evasive.

RITA (going and sitting on a tea-chest) I know. Tiger's asked me to go down to France with his mob.

FRANK Will you?

RITA I dunno. He's a bit of a wanker really. But I've never been abroad. An' me mother's invited me to hers for Christmas.

FRANK What are you going to do?

RITA I dunno. I might go to France. I might go to me mother's. I might even have a baby. I dunno. I'll make a decision, I'll choose. I dunno.

FRANK *has found a package hidden behind some of the books. He takes it down*

FRANK Whatever you do, you might as well take this …

RITA What?

FRANK *(handing it to her)* It's erm – well, it's er – it's a dress really. I bought it some time ago – for erm – for an educated woman friend – of mine …

RITA *takes the dress from the bag*

FRANK I erm – don't – know if it fits, I was rather pissed when I bought it …

RITA An educated woman, Frank? An' is this what you call a scholarly neckline?

FRANK When choosing it I put rather more emphasis on the word woman than the word educated.

RITA All I've ever done is take from you I've never given anything.

FRANK That's not true you've …

RITA It is true. I never thought there was anythin' I could give you. But there is. Come here, Frank…

FRANK What?

RITA Come here … *(She pulls out a chair)* Sit on that …

FRANK *is bewildered*

RITA Sit …

FRANK *sits and* RITA, *eventually finding a pair of scissors on the desk, waves them in the air*

RITA I'm gonna take ten years off you …

She goes across to him and begins to cut his hair. As she gets close to his ear-lobe FRANK *cries out 'Ouch'*

Black-out

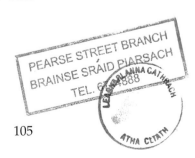

Further reading

All the books listed below are available as modern paperbacks and you will find most of them in your local library.

Other works by Willy Russell

Having read *Educating Rita*, you will probably be interested in reading other plays by Willy Russell. Three of his most popular plays are:

Shirley Valentine (1986), which features a character not unlike Rita. It was also, like *Educating Rita*, made into an immensely successful film.

Our Day Out (1977), a television play about a school trip and based on his experiences as a schoolteacher in a comprehensive in Liverpool.

Blood Brothers (1981), one of the most popular musical plays of recent times.

Other plays that he has written include:

John, Paul, George, Ringo and Bert (1974)

Breezeblock Park (1975)

One for the Road (1976)

Stags and Hens (1978)

Books with similar themes

There are two writers referred to in *Educating Rita* whose works deal with the same themes as the play:

Pygmalion (1914), a play by George Bernard Shaw tells the story of Eliza Doolittle, an uneducated cockney flower-seller. She encounters Professor Henry Higgins, who decides to try to 'educate' Eliza by changing her behaviour and the way she speaks and to establish her in upper-class society. There are obvious parallels between Shaw's play and Russell's, not least in the relationship between the pupil and the teacher. It formed the basis of the musical and film *My Fair Lady*.

Frankenstein is the other work referred to. Mary Shelley's novel, published in 1818, tells the story of a scientist who 'creates' a human being and brings it to life. Disastrous consequences follow when the creature becomes uncontrollable. Numerous films have been based on the book, but it's worth noting that they all exaggerate the 'monster-like' qualities of Victor Frankenstein's creation. Read the book and you will discover you are likely to have sympathy for the creature.

Other books referred to

Educating Rita refers to lots of other novels, plays and poems. Some of them you might find quite hard going, but you could try:

Howards End by E. M. Forster (1910), the first novel that Rita studies and which has parallels with the play.

Sons and Lovers by D. H. Lawrence (1913) is the most approachable of his novels and is the one that Rita defends in her argument with the students against the less successful *Lady Chatterley's Lover* (1928).

Of Human Bondage by Somerset Maugham (1915) is the novel Rita thought was about sexual perversion (it isn't!) and it might be worth a try.

The Importance of Being Earnest by Oscar Wilde (1895) is a very funny and witty play.

If you want to understand why Rita was confused about comedy and tragedy, Chekhov's plays *The Seagull* (1895) and *The Cherry Orchard* (1904) might be a good place to start, but they are not easy reading; if you haven't read or seen *Macbeth* then do so at once. Rita enjoyed it.

Of the major English poets Rita mentions, try:

Songs of Innocence and Experience by William Blake (1789 and 1794).

Lyrical Ballads by William Wordsworth (1798), which also includes Coleridge's famous poem *The Rime of the Ancient Mariner*.

You would certainly enjoy the Liverpool poets, Roger McGough and Adrian Henri, both of whom have similarities with Willy Russell's way of writing.

You'll have to decide for yourself if Rita Mae Brown's *Rubyfruit Jungle* is 'fantastic' (Rita: page 21) and 'excellent' (Frank: page 90) or 'of its type…quite interesting' (Rita: page 90).

Programme of study

1. Read the opening of the play to 'D' y' get a lot like me?' (page 15). In what ways is this extract a good introduction to the play's main characters and themes? Do you think Willy Russell has made his opening dramatic and entertaining?

2. Read Act 2 Scene 1 (pages 73–80) very carefully. How has the experience at summer school challenged Rita's view of the world and do you think that what follows is inevitable?

3. Referring to two scenes from *Educating Rita* show the different ways Willy Russell creates humour. In your answer you should refer to:
- the way the characters speak
- the way the characters behave
- the way the author develops situations
- the way the author uses irony.

4. In *Educating Rita* Willy Russell writes that 'education gives you a choice'. What changes are there in Rita as a result of her choosing education throughout the play? In your answer you should comment on changes
- in her background and culture
- in her personal circumstances
- in her personality.

5. Do you think Rita has gained or suffered as a result of her education?

6. Read Rita's speech on pages 47–8 that begins 'But they're not. Cos there's no meanin''. What does it reveal about her character, her ideas and her motivation? In what way is Frank's reaction to it important in her education?

7. Do Rita and Frank have anything in common? You should refer in your answer to:
- their relationship with their partners
- their feelings about their jobs
- any changes that take place within them
- what they have learned during the course of the play.

8. Referring to two scenes, one from each act, show how you would stage a performance of *Educating Rita* that reflected the changes in the characters and their attitudes to each other. You should write about:
- the costumes the characters would wear
- any changes to the set you might want to make
- how you would mark the passage of time.

9. If you have seen the film version of *Educating Rita*, write an essay about the reasons for the differences between the two versions and the effect the changes might have. You should write about:
- the setting and locations
- the number of characters we meet
- the changes in the plot
- scenes which appear in the film, but not in the play.

10. In what way is *Educating Rita* a play about the clash of class and culture?

Glossary

13 **Eliot:** T. S. Eliot (1888–1965) was one of the most important poets of the twentieth century
slug: a quantity of liquor that can be swallowed in one gulp

14 **Henry James:** an American novelist (1843–1916) who lived in England and whose books and ideas are seen as being very influential
ratatouille: a French vegetable stew

15 **erotic:** sexually stimulating

16 **embrace a more comprehensive studentship:** take in students from a wider range of ages and backgrounds
dubiously: doubtfully

17 **Dylan Thomas:** Welsh poet (1914–1953) who wrote a poem about facing death called *'Do not go gentle into that good night'*
Roger McGough: present-day poet from Liverpool, where Rita comes from
E. M. Foster: Rita's version of E. M. Forster: English novelist (1879–1970), whose novel *Howards End* tells a story that has some similarities to Rita's

18 **contemplating:** thinking about

19 **effin' an' blindin':** swearing
grouse: an expensive gamebird for eating

20 **assonance:** a form of rhyme in which the same vowel sounds are repeated
Yeats: W. B. Yeats (1865–1939), a very important Irish poet whose name is pronounced like *Yates*
wine lodge: a pub chain owned by a firm called Yates

21 **Rita Mae Brown:** American author of *Rubyfruit Jungle*, a sexually explicit novel

Frank Harris: English novelist (1856–1931) whose books were considered sexually daring and pornographic at the time they were written

Al Capone: the most famous Chicago gangster of the 1920s and 1930s who was finally caught by Elliott Ness

22   **J. Arthur Prufrock:** One of T. S. Eliot's best known poems is called *The Love Song of J. Alfred Prufrock*. Rita gets the name confused

23   **Farrah Fawcett Majors:** Glamorous and sexy American actress popular in the 1970s for her part in a television series called *Charlie's Angels*

Flora man: a man who featured in a well-known advertising campaign for Flora, promoted as a healthy low-fat spread

Flowers: the Latin for flowers is *flora*

pebble-dashed bread: Rita's joky term for wholemeal or wholegrain bread

24   **narked:** annoyed (slang)

25   **Formby:** an upper middle-class town north of Liverpool

26   **Wilde:** Oscar Wilde (1854–1900) was an Irish playwright famous for very witty remarks

geriatric hippie: in the 1960s, hippies rejected society's traditional values and sought an alternative lifestyle; they wore flower-power clothes, used soft drugs and often had long and wild hairstyles. 'Geriatric' here means old and outdated

30   **patina:** the surface appearance; here Rita is referring to the untidy appearance of Frank's book-lined room which seems to reflect his personality

30   **tuck shop:** a shop in a public or private school where pupils buy sweets and small items of food

31   **matron:** the woman who looks after the health of pupils in a public or private school

prep: public school term for homework

Jones minor...major: major and minor were the words used to distinguish an elder from a younger brother in a public school where pupils are called by their surnames only

Isabel Archer: the heroine of Henry James' novel, *The Portrait of a Lady*

protestant masochism: masochism is the willingness to endure pain, often for the sexual thrill it brings. Here it is being associated with people who follow the Protestant religious faith

32   **Jane Austen:** (1775–1816) very famous English novelist who wrote *Pride and Prejudice*

Tracy Austin: American tennis player of the 1980s

33   **appreciation:** a review of a book that says only complimentary and positive things

purely objective: not including any personal opinions or prejudices, but being as neutral as possible

established literary critique: the way or tradition that other critics have written about literature

subjective: the opposite of objective; writing only from a personal and possibly biased point of view

partisan interpretation: very biased view

sentiment: excessive feeling

F. R. Leavis: very influential English literary critic (1895–1978) who taught at Cambridge University

34   **ivory tower:** a metaphor for people who are remote from the interests and concerns of ordinary people

Marxist viewpoint: critics who look at a work of literature from a point of view influenced by the ideas of Karl Marx, the Communist thinker. They stress the influence of the social and economic conditions at the time the book was written

immoral: knowing what is right, but still behaving wrongly

Amoral: having no understanding of right or wrong

Brevity: shortness

35 *conspiratorially*: as if plotting or scheming

36 **a detailed knowledge of the literary references:** to understand Frank's poetry you would need a detailed knowledge of other literary works

38 **'only connect':** this is the most famous phrase from *Howards End*. E. M. Forster means that it is vital for people to understand and relate to each other

41 *flounces*: walks impatiently

Harold Robbins: an American popular novelist, one of whose books is *A Stone for Danny Fisher*. His books are not well thought of by traditional literary critics

pulp fiction: fiction that is popular, but thought to be trivial and sensational by some academic critics

42 *Sons and Lovers*: a novel by the English writer, D. H. Lawrence (1874–1930)

perverted: Rita thinks that the title of the novel *Of Human Bondage* sounds as if the book is about unusual sexual activities. It isn't!

Noel Coward: (1899–1973) English playwright, actor and composer who, like Somerset Maugham, was a homosexual

Somerset Maugham: (1874–1965) English novelist who wrote *Of Human Bondage*

43 **discerning:** having good judgement

slap an' tickle: slang sexual play. Rita compares reading pulp fiction to having a bit of slap and tickle. It's enjoyable, but not something you tell everyone about

44 *Peer Gynt*: a very long play by Henrik Ibsen (1828–1906), a Norwegian dramatist. It is not performed on stage very frequently, because it is difficult to stage

resolve: overcome

inherent: existing in, inseparable from

45   **naïve:** foolish, simple

considered: thoughtful

encapsulated: condensed

exquisite: beautiful, excellent

46   **accepted authorities:** critics whose opinions are highly valued

47   **Valium:** a tranquilliser

keg beer: beer kept in metal containers, thought to be of inferior quality to real beer

51   **wearisome:** tedious

Chekhov: Anton Chekhov (1860–1904) was a Russian dramatist

library steps: movable set of steps that allows you to reach the highest shelves of books

52   **cryin' over spilt milk:** (proverb) there is no point in getting upset over something that has already happened

53   **rockin' the coffin:** upsetting their present pattern of life

Stork: brand of margarine

54   **stashed:** stored

discretion: acting carefully

55   **that Chekhov play:** *The Seagull*, a comedy by Chekhov in which Constantin is a major character. Rita cannot understand why it is called a comedy; Frank tries to explain to her

stand-up comedy: a comic routine delivered by just one comedian standing in front of an audience and telling jokes

ravishing: very attractive

ludicrous: silly, laughable

M.A.: university degree (Master of Arts)

56   ***The Importance of Bein' Thingy:*** Rita's version of the title of Oscar Wilde's famous and very witty comedy, *The Importance of Being Earnest*

aghast: horrified

60 **Out, out, brief candle!:** Rita quotes one of the most famous speeches from *Macbeth*, but Frank then pretends that it's from *Romeo and Juliet*

invincible: unconquerable

perm lotion: treatment to make hair curly

61 **it's that flaw … his own doom:** Frank explains that in tragedy the hero has a weakness (or flaw) of character that will inevitably lead to his death or downfall

inevitable: unavoidable

pre-ordained: arranged beforehand either by the gods or because of the hero's unchangeable character

62 **demi-wave:** hair treatment which makes hair go wavy but not curly

muppet: popular television puppets of the time with wild hairstyles

65 **vino:** informal word for wine

stage-manager type: the stage manager in the theatre prepares the stage, props and scenery to ensure the play runs without any problems. In the same way, Julia organises dinner parties very carefully

66 **Shaw:** George Bernard Shaw (1856–1950) was an Irish playwright. 'Shavian' is the adjective used to describe his works

plonk: an informal word for low quality wine

67 **comin' on with the funnies:** telling jokes

court jester: a clown paid to entertain the king and queen and the nobility

analyst: psychoanalyst: someone who diagnoses and attempts to cure mental and emotional problems

paranoia: mental illness in which you feel victimised or persecuted by everybody

half-caste: someone whose parents are of different races. Rita means that she feels she belongs neither to the type of people at Frank's dinner party nor to the people she grew up and lives with

69   **ultimatum:** last offer or demand

       warped: twisted out of shape, distorted

71   **suppress:** check, hold back

       uniqueness: what makes a person entirely different from anyone else

73   **summer school:** an academic course for Open University students held at a university during the summer holidays when the regular students are away

74   **Ferlinghetti:** Lawrence Ferlinghetti (1919–) is a famous and influential modern American poet

       Parmesan cheese: an Italian cheese, often sprinkled over pasta. The name, Ferlinghetti, sounded like an Italian dish, but she stopped herself from making the obvious joke

       Gauloise: the most typical French brand of cigarette

75   *oeufs en cocotte,* **Florentine, Benedict,** *Oeufs à la Crécy:* all these are different and stylish ways of serving eggs

76   **Dracula:** the legendary count, reputed to be a vampire

       aversion: strong dislike for (vampires are said to die if exposed to sunlight)

77   **analogy:** comparison

       cuttings: small piece of a plant cut off to encourage it to develop into a new plant

       germinate: raise a new plant from a seed

78   **frantic whirl:** never ending series of events

       sobriety: being sober

79   **mortuary:** place where dead bodes are stored

       Blake: William Blake (1757–1827) was an English poet, artist and revolutionary thinker whose most famous poem is *The Sick Rose*

       Blake freak: someone obsessed with Blake's work

80	**Parody ... humour:** a parody is a piece of writing imitating the style of an author, usually to make fun of it

80   **Parody ... humour:** a parody is a piece of writing imitating the style of an author, usually to make fun of it
masquerading: pretending to be, disguising itself as

83   **Dalek:** robot with a monotonous electronic voice that appeared in the TV series *Dr Who*

84   **wary:** very cautious about
***Lady Chatterley, Sons and Lovers*:** Two novels by the English novelist D. H. Lawrence

85   **slummin' it:** living as cheaply as possible
burbling on: never stopping talking

86   *tome:* large book
rostrum: platform from which speakers address their audience
misdemeanour: minor offence
bursar: finance officer of the university
sabbatical: paid leave for academic staff to do research
allusion: an indirect remark or reference. Frank is referring to the time when British convicts were transported to Australia

87   **mealy-mouthed:** smooth-talking
desecrated: vandalised
Wordsworth: William Wordsworth (1770–1850) was a very important English poet
'The Blossom': poem by William Blake

88   **simple surface value:** the immediate meaning of the poem

93   **bistro:** small, informal, continental style restaurant

95   **literary criticism:** writing objectively about literary texts

96   **reasonable comprehension:** able to understand what is being said
profound: full of deep meaning
resonant: full of echoes and allusions to earlier literary works and styles
wit: clever ideas or word play

classical allusion: references to Greek and Roman history and myths

97 **Mary Shelley:** author (1797–1851) of the novel *Frankenstein* in which a scientist, Victor Frankenstein, creates a living creature that he is unable to control. Frank is implying that he has created this 'new' Rita and that he no longer has any influence over her

Gothic number: *Frankenstein* is a type of novel known as 'Gothic'. Such novels were full of suspense, horror and strange supernatural incidents

pyrotechnical: superficial, flashy, lasting only a short time (like fireworks)

hallmark: a guarantee of quality. Hallmarks are usually stamped on things made from gold or silver

98 **squanders:** wastes

pretentious: meaning very little, though written in a superficially impressive way

Virginia, Charlotte, Jane, Emily: references to literary writers: Virginia Woolf, Charlotte and Emily Brontë, Jane Austen

101 *denote*: indicate

102 *tea-chests*: large packing cases used when moving house

Metaphorically: Frank means he didn't literally 'bugger the bursar'

Bon voyage: French for 'have a good journey'

103 **Forster's Lager:** Frank jokes about Foster's lager, a favourite drink of Australians. Rita earlier pronounced E. M. Forster as E. M. Foster

invigilator: someone who supervises an examination

top herself: informal expression for committing suicide

104 **jumpin' a sinkin' ship:** leaving the ship which is sinking rather than staying aboard and trying to save it. Rita means that the ship is England

evasive: avoiding the question

Title list

NEW LONGMAN LITERATURE

Post-1914 Fiction

0 582 43446 7	I'm the King of the Castle	Susan Hill
0 582 02660 1	The Woman in Black	Susan Hill
0 582 25399 3	The Mist in the Mirror	Susan Hill
0 582 06016 8	Brave New World	Aldous Huxley
0 582 06017 6	The Cone-Gatherers	Robin Jenks
0 582 06021 4	The Fifth Child	Doris Lessing
0 582 08174 2	Picnic at Hanging Rock	Joan Lindsay
0 582 06557 7	Lamb	Bernard MacLaverty
0 582 08170 X	Lies of Silence	Brian Moore
0 582 43447 5	Animal Farm	George Orwell
0 582 06023 0	The Great Gatsby	F Scott-Fitzgerald
0 582 46146 4	Of Mice and Men	John Steinbeck
0 582 46147 2	The Pearl	John Steinbeck
0 582 46149 9	The Moon is Down	John Steinbeck
0 582 46150 2	Tortilla Flat	John Steinbeck
0 582 46151 0	Cannery Row	John Steinbeck
0 582 46152 9	East of Eden	John Steinbeck
0 582 46153 7	The Grapes of Wrath	John Steinbeck
0 582 43448 3	Daz 4 Zoe	Robert Swindells
0 582 29247 6	A Slipping Down Life	Anne Tyler
0 582 09714 2	To the Lighthouse	Virginia Woolf

Post-1914 Short Stories

0 582 28730 8	Quartet of Stories
0 582 23369 0	The Human Element & Other Stories
0 582 43449 1	A Roald Dahl Selection
0 582 28931 9	Stories Old and New
0 582 03922 3	Stories from Asia
0 582 25393 4	Stories from Africa
0 582 28928 9	Mystery and Horror
0 582 28927 0	War Stories
0 582 02661 X	Ghost Stories
0 582 28929 7	Global Tales
0 582 29249 2	Ten D H Lawrence Short Stories

Post-1914 Poetry

0 582 29248 4	Voices of the Great War
0 582 35149 9	Poetry 1900 to 1975

| 0 582 25401 9 | Poems 2 | |

Post-1914 Plays

0 582 30242 0	Absent Friends	Alan Ayckbourn
0 582 06019 2	The Winslow Boy	Terrence Rattigan
0 582 22389 X	P'Tang, Yang, Kipperbang & other TV plays	Jack Rosenthal
0 582 43445 9	Educating Rita	Willy Russell
0 582 08173 4	Shirley Valentine	Willy Russell
0 582 25383 7	Ten Short Plays	
0 582 25394 2	Scenes from Plays	
0 582 06014 1	The Royal Hunt of the Sun	Peter Shaffer
0 582 09712 6	Equus	Peter Shaffer
0 582 06015 X	Pygmalion	Bernard Shaw
0 582 07786 9	Saint Joan	Bernard Shaw
0 582 25396 9	The Rivals/The School for Scandal	Richard Brinsley Sheridan

Post-1914 Stories from other Cultures

0 582 28730 8	Quartet of Stories	
0 582 06011 7	July's People	Nadine Gordimer
0 582 25398 5	Heat and Dust	Ruth Prawer Jhabvala
0 582 07787 7	Cry, the Beloved Country	Alan Paton
0 582 03922 3	Stories from Asia	
0 582 25393 4	Stories from Africa	
0 582 28929 7	Global Tales	

Post-1914 Non-Fiction

0 582 25391 8	Genres	
0 582 25384 5	Diaries and Letters	
0 582 28932 7	Introducing Media	
0 582 25386 1	Travel Writing	
0 582 08837 2	Autobiographies	
0 582 01736 X	The Diary of Anne Frank	

Pre-1914 Fiction

0 582 07720 6	Pride and Prejudice	Jane Austen
0 582 07719 2	Jane Eyre	Charlotte Brontë
0 582 07782 6	Wuthering Heights	Emily Brontë
0 582 07783 4	Great Expectations	Charles Dickens
0 582 28729 4	Oliver Twist	Charles Dickens
0 582 23664 9	A Christmas Carol	Charles Dickens
0 582 23662 2	Silas Marner	George Eliot
0 582 22586 8	The Mayor of Casterbridge	Thomas Hardy
0 582 07788 5	Far from the Madding Crowd	Thomas Hardy
0 582 30244 7	Ethan Frome	Edith Wharton

Pre-1914 Collections

0 582 25405 1	Wessex Tales	Thomas Hardy
0 582 28931 9	Stories Old and New	
0 582 28927 0	War Stories	
0 582 25388 8	Characters from Pre-20th Century Novels	
0 582 25384 5	Diaries and Letters	
0 582 25385 3	Highlights from 19th Century Novels	
0 582 25389 6	Landmarks	
0 582 25386 1	Travel Writing	
0 582 33807 7	19th Century Short Stories of Passion & Mystery	

Pre-1914 Poetry

0 582 22585 X	Poems from Other Centuries	

Pre-1914 Plays

0 582 25397 7	She Stoops to Conquer	Oliver Goldsmith
0 582 24948 1	Three Plays	Henrik Ibsen
0 582 25409 4	Doctor Faustus	Christopher Marlowe
0 582 28930 0	Starting Shakespeare	
0 582 43444 0	The Devil's Disciple	Bernard Shaw
0 582 07785 0	Arms and the Man	Bernard Shaw
0 582 28731 6	The Duchess of Malfi	John Webster
0 582 07784 2	The Importance of Being Earnest	Oscar Wilde

NEW CENTURY READERS

Post-1914 Contemporary Fiction

0 582 32847 0	Granny the Pag	Nina Bawden
0 582 29254 9	The Real Plato Jones	Nina Bawden
0 582 25395 0	A Question of Courage	Marjorie Darke
0 582 32845 4	Daughter of the Sea	Berlie Doherty
0 582 43455 6	The Snake Stone	Berlie Doherty
0 582 29262 X	My Family and other Natural Disasters	Josephine Feeney
0 582 31941 2	The Tulip Touch	Anne Fine
0 582 43452 1	Flour Babies	Anne Fine
0 582 29257 3	A Pack of Liars	Anne Fine
0 582 29258 1	The Book of the Banshee	Anne Fine
0 582 29261 1	Madame Doubtfire	Anne Fine
0 582 29251 4	Step by Wicked Step	Anne Fine
0 582 29260 3	Goggle Eyes	Anne Fine
0 582 29255 7	MapHead	Lesley Howarth

0 582 43453 X	A Northern Childhood	George Layton
0 582 32846 2	Lizzie's Leaving	Joan Lingard
0 582 31967 6	Night Fires	Joan Lingard
0 582 43456 4	Goodnight Mister Tom	Michelle Magorian
0 582 43451 3	Journey to Jo'burg	Beverley Naidoo
0 582 36419 1	Aquila	Andrew Norriss
0 582 29256 5	Along a Lonely Road	Catherine Sefton
0 582 46148 0	The Red Pony	John Steinbeck
0 582 31966 8	A Serpent's Tooth	Robert Swindells
0 582 31968 4	Follow a Shadow	Robert Swindells
0 582 31964 1	Urn Burial	Robert Westall

Post-1914 Poetry

0 582 25400 0	Poems 1
0 582 22587 6	Poems in my Earphone

Post-1914 Plays

0 582 43450 5	Mirad, a Boy from Bosnia	Ad de Bont
0 582 09556 5	Bill's New Frock	Anne Fine
0 582 09555 7	Collision Course	Nigel Hinton
0 582 09554 9	Maid Marian and her Merry Men	Tony Robinson
0 582 10156 5	The Fwog Prince	Kaye Umansky

Pre-1914

0 582 42944 7	Oliver Twist	Charles Dickens
0 582 29253 0	Twisters